Bigmama Didn't Shop at Woolworth's

Sunny Nash
7-22-98

A WARDLAW BOOK

Bigmama
DIDN'T SHOP AT
Woolworth's

SUNNY NASH

TEXAS A&M UNIVERSITY PRESS
COLLEGE STATION

The paper used in this book meets the minimum requirements
of the American National Standard for Permanence
of Paper for Printed Library Materials, Z39.48-1984.
Binding materials have been chosen for durability.

Library of Congress Cataloging-in-Publication Data

Nash, Sunny, 1949–

  Bigmama didn't shop at Woolworth's / by Sunny Nash. — 1st. ed.

    p.   cm. — (A wardlaw book)

  ISBN 0-89096-716-4 (cloth : alk. paper)

  1. Nash, Sunny, 1949–   —Childhood and youth. 2. Afro-American women—
Texas—Bryan—Biography. 3. Afro-Americans—Texas—Bryan—Biography. 4. Afro-
Americans—Segregation—Texas—Bryan. 5. Bryan (Tex.)—Biography. I. Title.
II. Series.

F394.B94N37   1996

976.4´242—dc20   96-14743

                                                                                          CIP

To my mother and father

Littie & Henry Nash

And in memory of my grandmother

Edna Minor Gibbs

Contents

Illustrations

Acknowledgments

Many thanks to my newspaper editor and friend, Ken Hammond, of the *Texas Magazine* of the *Houston Chronicle,* for always asking me to dig a little deeper.

Special appreciation to my friend and fellow author, David Westheimer, for years of encouragement.

Much gratitude to my Candy Hill neighbors, without whom there would have been no material for this book.

Publisher's Acknowledgment

The Texas A&M University Press is privileged to add its imprint to this Wardlaw Book. The designation claims a special place in the list of Texas A&M publications.

Supported with funds inspired by the initiative of Chester Kerr, former head of Yale University Press, this book, along with its companion volumes, perpetuates the association of Frank H. Wardlaw's name with a select group of titles appropriate to his reputation as a man of letters, distinguished publisher, and founder of three university presses.

Donors of these funds represent a wide cross-section of Frank Wardlaw's admirers, including colleagues from scholarly presses throughout the country as well as those from other callings who recognize and applaud the many contributions that he has made to scholarship, literature, and publishing in his four decades of active service.

The Texas A&M University Press acknowledges with profound appreciation these donors.

Mr. Herbert S. Bailey, Jr.   Mr. Kenneth Johnson
Mr. Robert Barnes   Mr. Chester Kerr
Mr. W. Walker Cowen   Mr. Robert T. King
Mr. Robert S. Davis   Mr. Carl C. Krueger, Jr.
Mr. John Ervin, Jr.   Mr. John H. Kyle
Mr. William D. Fitch   John and Sara Lindsey
Mr. August Frugé   Mrs. S. M. McAshan, Jr.
Mr. David H. Gilbert   Mr. Kenneth E. Montague

Mr. Edward J. Mosher

Mrs. Florence Rosengren

Mr. Jack Schulman

Mr. C. B. Smith

Mr. Richard A. Smith

Mr. Stanley Sommers

Dr. Frank E. Vandiver

Ms. Maud E. Wilcox

Mr. John Williams

Their bounty has assured that Wardlaw Books will be a special source of instruction and entertainment to the reading public for many years to come.

Introduction

Despite the imagery suggested by the name Candy Hill, in the 1950s there was little that was sweet or playful about the maze of unpaved roads, narrow trails, and mosquito-infested drainage ditches that led to and from the neighborhood's rows of mostly shotgun houses with outdoor toilets. Beer flowed night and day at corner joints, making their owners across town rich. After hours, Candy Hill men and women staggered home with mean dispositions, drunken tempers flaring frequently and violently. Folks who quietly accepted low social status beat, cut, and shot each other on Saturday nights. Others went to church on Sunday and prayed for their children's escape or improvement.

Superficially accepting denigration, a makeshift life, and the task of holding up a road on which others were privileged to ride, Candy Hill people secretly planted ambitions in the minds of their sons and daughters. Generation after generation, humble parents hoped for change and optimistically created expectations far beyond those allowed by society.

With no silver spoon in my mouth, I was descended equally from the legacies of African bondage and Amerindian freedom. In what was racially the least stable period in America's existence, I inherited a burden of negative history from my varied ancestors. Along with that burden, my shoulders bore responsibility for elevating future generations of my people. Further, my plight included changing the attitudes of everyone who has in the past or will in the future contribute to the spiritually wounded condition of my oppressed and violated ancestors. These expectations my family passed to me. I accepted their virtues and code of civilized behavior, though not always without question or complaint.

Elegant and gracious, my mother believed that the human condition could be raised by individual development—through reading, music, art, dance, conversation, travel. Teaching me respect for others, dignity, impeccable manners, and correct speech, she tried to make me feel comfortable being genteel in a nation that promised me at birth that these qualities would guarantee me nothing. "Read a book because you want to know something," she said. "Be intelligent because it's better than being ignorant."

My grandmother, as wise a person as I've ever known, had a global view of the human condition. "The only way the world will change for the better is that everybody in the world gets tired of things being messed up," she said. "And there's not much chance of that happening."

My father's approach to changing human condition was practical. "Get you some green in your pocket," he said. "Use that green to get some more green. Because when America stops understanding black, brown, red, yellow, and white, it will still understand green."

Physical freedom left Candy Hill parents locked firmly in psychological chains placed there by racists who never had been emancipated from an illusion of superiority. Their illusion affected all aspects of our lives—earning a living, education, going to a movie, medical care, purchasing property, shopping for groceries, voting, and travel. The common thought on Candy Hill was: If we are so mentally inferior, what supports the need to spy, write laws, and pass judgments to the detriment of people so inept?

Constant scrutiny by outsiders of activities on Candy Hill forced residents to use secret codes of communication comprised of subtle eye movements, slight hand gestures, body language, and redefined terms or slang that changed when definitions became known outside the group. These carefully crafted techniques of trickery and social masking were not designed to pass complicated messages concerning civil revolution or international subversion. There were no such notions on Candy Hill. The mysterious language was invented simply for privacy.

Unable to decipher the code, an insecure and suspicious ruling class passed and severely enforced laws against us to erect economic obstacles with which to buttress racial barriers. These traditional economic roadblocks kept Candy Hill people from achieving a decent life and participating in the mainstream. For decades, Candy Hill mothers and fathers were forced to separate or abandon their families and play other dangerous domestic games in order to qualify for stigmatizing social benefits. Beaten into submission by job insecurity, fear of physical violence, and threat of starvation, Candy Hill families watched on television as the civil rights movement rose and fell in the 1960s and as the promise of social change died on disco floors in the 1970s, much like affirmative action is dying on government floors today. So goes existence on Candy Hill, once again passed over by the good life.

Bigmama Didn't Shop at Woolworth's

1

◆

Blood Relations

Movies —
Not Just Black-and-White

My mother took me downtown to lunch and my first Saturday movie matinee when I was four years old.

That was in 1953.

It looked like rain that morning, but I begged my mother to go to the movies anyway. She finally agreed. So we got all dressed up in our Sunday clothes and combed our hair in styles reserved for special occasions.

We left the house singing and holding hands, while the sun played cat-and-mouse with tumbling clouds. For the first three or four blocks, we labored on gravel near our house, careful not to scuff our black patent-leather shoes. After leaving Candy Hill and reaching a neighborhood with smooth pavement, sidewalks, and fine lawns, we strolled easily the rest of the way.

"Is this downtown yet?" I asked.

"No," she said. "When we get to downtown, you'll see lots of stores with pretty things in the windows."

The houses were soon behind us. Buildings lined the streets. Excitement at seeing our reflections in the glass made me forget about my aching feet. Our first stop was for burgers at a greasy cafe on the lower end of Main Street. We walked around the block to the rear door of the establishment that faced Bryan Street.

"When we go inside, be quiet," my mother said. "You can't have a drink because there's no restroom that we can use."

The strong smells of a well-seasoned grill and fresh raw onions stung my nostrils as we stood at the counter for a long time. Through the front door, others came in after we were there and were served promptly. Finally, the large rude cook took our order and demanded money before he prepared the food.

Without reply, my mother dug into her tiny cloth coin purse and paid. Time passed as slowly as it could before her change and our food arrived. "Y'all can't eat in here," the cook said.

Without a word, my mother grabbed my hand and dragged me to the back door. As we stood outside and ate in silence, I thought I saw a tear sparkle on my mother's cheek as that day's last sunlight stroked her face.

With a few drops of rain falling on us, we took the short walk to the Palace Theater and stood at the ticket window outside the main lobby. The aroma of buttered popcorn floated through the little round hole in the glass where the ticket woman worked.

To avoid getting wet in the shower, other moviegoers dashed through a glass front door into the dry, comfortable lobby filled with tiny white lights, velvet drapery, and red carpet. By the time my mother and I got our tickets, big drops of rain were splashing down on our heads. With her hair, heavy with water, sliding into her face, my mother dug into her tiny cloth coin purse and paid.

The little blue door on the outside of the theater slammed us into the darkest place I'd ever been—like a coffin, I thought, holding my mother's hand. We stumbled up stairs too steep for my short legs to a musty, unlit balcony. As my mother pulled me to a seat, I glanced over the low balcony wall and saw heads of shiny hair cascading over upholstered chairs.

My mother unfolded for me a worn seat with splintering veneer armrests. Exhausted, I let the chair fold me up a little. To the sounds of the thunderstorm, I dropped off to sleep before the opening credits flashed across the screen.

Faces on
Dark Thrones

I walked into the darkened bedroom through a blistered doorway that, in 1954, when I was only five years old, seemed very tall to me. Inside the room, heavy draperies sagged from two narrow floor-to-ceiling windows, sealed shut so long ago that several seasons of dead houseflies lined their sills. My Great-Aunt Sis said the carpenters had painted the windows shut when they worked on her house back in the forties. But, according to my grandmother, Aunt Sis had lied about the windows. Bigmama said the windows were not painted shut at all. Aunt Sis had ordered the workmen to nail them shut because she was afraid. Afraid of what, I asked.

"Everything!" Bigmama said. "Her own shadow, owl hoots, and even night falling."

"Why?"

"Some of my people have lived three generations with one eye over their shoulder," she said. "Fear is bred in prairie blood, always on the run. Afraid the ghost of some old dead soldier will pop out their eyes and lock them up in a pen. Sis passed that awful curse to my children, since she has none of her own. But fear can't take over a body unless a body gives in to it."

Aunt Sis didn't come to visit us on Candy Hill anymore after she took my great-grandfather into her home. "I have no choice," I overheard her say to my grandmother. "You can't take him. Y'all are as cramped as sardines, always taking in this one and that one with no-

*Bigmama (Edna Minor Gibbs) with Sunny Nash's mother
(Littie Gibbs Nash) at age one, 1929.*

where else to go. Where would you put him? And Leatha can't take him. She's sick and blind. And crazy Dan would never allow it anyway."

"Pretty woman like that could have done so much better than mean, stingy Dan," said Bigmama.

"Effie and her mob of grandchildren live like wandering vagabonds, drifting from one relative to another all summer," Aunt Sis said. "I've got this big old house and nothing much to do. I'll take him."

I missed Aunt Sis's visits and shuddering late at night, after she got to drinking, when she told spooky prairie tales about the family. She was more frightened by, and laughed harder at, her own haunted humor than anyone listening. Gold crowns on her upper front teeth sparkled under the kitchen light; her dimpled cheeks swelled up and hid her eyes; and her huge lumpy bosom bounced like a four-hundred-pound shelf of bed pillows.

"Don't be scared," whispered Aunt Sis, not her usual jolly self, standing just inside the bedroom door and nudging me gently farther into the room, toward what looked like an enormous throne on the opposite wall. I studied it more carefully. It was a bed. "That's your great-grandfather lying over there."

Squinting, my eyes had no difficulty seeing that there was no movement in the bed. Startled by the lifeless lump, I jumped back, rejecting my great-grandfather and his musty quarters that never got a breeze. The still, damp, stale coolness of his room was not like the pleasant temperature of a spring morning or the crispness of sitting on the back of the ice wagon or a red Popsicle frosty feeling or the chill of cold sweat running off the butter churn or the first day of fall. Nor did the climate of my great-grandfather's room resemble that of the machine-cooled air in Woolworth's Five-and-Dime, Edge's Dress Shop, or Humpty-Dumpty Grocery, where I'd been with my mother.

Could Aunt Sis's house possibly retain cold air throughout the year, I wondered, returning to the skin-crawling conditions of my great-grandfather's room. No. Last winter, when Bigmama and I visited, the house had been quite hot. Dry logs had crackled in the fireplace, and more heat billowed from the kitchen, where Aunt Sis prepared a tasteless boiled meal. No. This was a different kind of cool than little pieces of winter trapped between walls. Besides, no cold wind blew in around Aunt Sis's nailed windows or tight doors, unlike our drafty house. At a certain time on cold winter days, my mother's rag-stuffing ritual began. Everybody wanting in for the night had to be in before rags went into the cracks around the doors. No amount of begging would convince her to undo this work. I stuffed an old sock into the hole under my bed one winter until Sugar Ray's greyhounds were messing around under there and pulled it out.

My great-grandfather's clammy mixture of exhaled air and odors of liniment, dead wooden furniture, Oriental carpet, and flowers cut fresh from beds in Aunt Sis's yard conjured up in my mind images of a funeral home. I started remembering stories that my older cousins had told about Aunt Sis's last husband. They'd said he died in this very house. I was too young to know if that was true or not. They said Aunt Sis had had some neighbor men prepare and lay his body in the living room on a cooling board, a swinging door they took down from the dining room. My cousins said Aunt Sis invited everybody in Anderson to come by and gawk at him, and the quiet gathering soon modulated into a big farewell bash. Eating too much crackling bread, hog brains, and eggs and getting drunk on homemade beer, everybody ended up staying overnight and slobbering sentimental good-byes to the body. Bigmama said that's what Aunt Sis wanted, because she'd never knowingly have stayed alone in a house with a dead body, husband or not.

"Go over and let your great-grandfather see you, child," Aunt Sis said again, nudging me closer to the bed where the old man half sat and half laid in the middle of a semicircle of pillows against the tall black headboard. Carved figures of humanlike animal faces strained against the dark wood and gazed out of colorless eyeballs. The shapes of leaves and roses protruded from wood, crowning the top of the massive structure like a throne, holding my great-grandfather.

Family portraits, vases of flowers, cut-glass knickknacks, and ceramic whatnots—neatly arranged on shelves and bureau surfaces atop stiffened lace doilies—surrounded him. On each side of the bed, lace-covered tables held frosted hurricane lamps. Small bulbs and dangling crystal teardrop prisms reflected light off the shine of the old man's blue-blackness. With adjusted vision, my eyes stared at light glimmering against his long straight nose and balancing on each of his high sharp cheekbones. Long black hair was matted past his shoulders. Small, dingy, motionless eyes seemed to stare straight through me.

"Is he dead?" my whisper echoed.

"Lord, I hope not!" Aunt Sis screeched.

"Ain't dead yet!" his razor-thin lips roared.

Feeling sorry for himself and punishing Aunt Sis for keeping him alive, the old man wouldn't let his daughters or any of God's nicest angels put soap and water to him. I overheard my mother say that her grandfather's condition had really changed him. There had been a time, she said, when he was the picture of good grooming. "His shirts were so white it hurt your eyes to look at him in the sun." As he lay helpless among rumpled sheets, his uncut toenails pushed against the underside of the sheet.

He didn't remind me of any old people I knew on Candy Hill. One old lady we called Aunt Gnat had lost her teeth so long ago she hardly had gums. Did having no teeth stop her from eating? No! That old lady ate everything—soft or hard, cooked or raw, living or dead. She cracked bones faster than Sugar Ray's dogs. She said she didn't need teeth and didn't want anybody pretending to take care of her by running her business. All she needed was the Lord! With the Lord, she said, she could gum herself all the way to hell and eat every roasted body down there, including the Devil himself!

Hallelujah!

One old toothless Candy Hill man I knew took two-inch steps everywhere he went, whether it was around the house or around the block. Did two-inch steps stop that old man from walking? No! Every day he toddled up to the corner beer joint and bought himself a quart of Grand Prize. Some days, the two-block trip took that old man half a day.

My great-grandfather seemed to have most of his teeth; and, like Aunt Gnat, he could have had the Lord. Aunt Gnat said anybody—young or old, man or woman, black or white, rich or poor—can have the Lord! The Lord is free! Old Preacher Manley hated to hear that "Lord is free" talk. It interfered with the collection plate on Sunday. Aunt Gnat said she wouldn't be caught dead in a church house. No lying preacher man is going to tell her she can't get into Heaven unless she slaps a quarter on the collection table so he can put in a good word with the Lord on her behalf. Yes, there were plenty of old Candy Hill people in worse shape than my great-grandfather, and they weren't lying around praying to die.

"Go over and let your great-grandfather see you," Aunt Sis said nervously, like she'd never told a joke in her life.

"Can't that gal hear?" he yelled. "I can't hear, but I ain't supposed to be able to hear. I'm old!"

"I can hear," I said softly.

"He wants to see you up close." Aunt Sis stood behind me, smoothing my hair.

"I don't like him," I said softly.

"Speak up, gal!" he roared.

"I said, I don't like you!" I yelled. "Don't like nothing about you. The way you look. The way you smell. The way you keep hollering at me like you can't hear and I know you can. The way you're laying up there feeling sorry for yourself. I don't like nothing about you! Nothing!"

Private Business

On her way out of our three-room duplex going to my great-grandfather's funeral, Bigmama turned to me and said, "You stay home with your mother and your brother. Your great-grandfather will not miss you."

Aunt Sis had told the entire family about my visit. None of them knew how I agonized over the way I'd treated the old man. But his disregard for life offended me! Praying to die seemed almost as bad to me as someone trying to kill himself. How was I supposed to know that my great-grandfather lived by something my grandmother called "the old prairie way"? My great-grandfather accepted praying for the death of the old and ill to make room for the young and healthy.

"Would you want to be a burden on people?" Bigmama asked. "And lie around not able to move?"

"No," I said, ashamed.

"Be useless and can't do for yourself?"

"No."

While my last "no" hung in the air, my grandmother walked out. The frayed screen door slammed behind her. I followed her, closed the door softly, and sat down on the step. Her brother-in-law George—a jet-black gentleman cowboy with one of the few cars in the family—waited for her out front in his shiny black Buick. When he was young, Uncle George broke horses and punched cattle on the Yeager Ranch near Iola. He'd retired years before but still lived in a cabin on the ranch, and the Yeagers made sure he had a new car every two years or so. Before I was born, he was married to Bigmama's sister Lill, until her death. Uncle George never remarried. He got out of the car and opened the trunk for Bigmama's suitcase. His sweet-smelling cologne drifted from the street to my nose. As usual, he wore a crisp white dress shirt, gray pin-striped suit, cream Stetson hat, and fancy cowboy boots.

"Come on, Wideface," Uncle George called from the car to my grandmother. He said Wideface was Bigmama's Comanche name. I don't know which annoyed her more—being called by the name or being identified with the group.

"If you weren't as black as midnight," she called to him, "you'd be a white man. Stuff that in your pipe and suck on it."

I don't think Uncle George and my grandmother liked each other very much. If they did, it didn't show. Without another word, they got into the car and drove away.

For the first time, my mother was alone with her little children— me and my terminally ill brother, Johnny. My brother's health was a constant source of guilt to my mother, and she spent every waking moment caring for him. Although I never doubted her love for me, my primary care came from my grandmother, whom I missed after she left for the old man's funeral. Our matchbook-thin walls seemed less secure without Bigmama, because my mother, like Aunt Sis, lived with one eye over her shoulder like a woman being punished, expecting the worst. Both women tried to latch, lock, bolt, brace, chain, and nail out danger.

Under the shade of the hackberry tree on the front steps, I waited every day, hoping that Uncle George's Buick would come down our dirt road. My grandmother couldn't call us with her schedule. That was before we had a telephone. This lack of communication also caused a steady stream of penniless pregnant cousins, sick uncles, old aunts, and abandoned friends to arrive unannounced, giving me lots of interesting details of private business to overhear. Mysteriously, our house expanded to shelter whatever number of us there happened to be at the time.

Occasionally, someone wrote a letter that arrived days after they did. That was the style of Aunt Effie, Bigmama's sister, when she showed up for her routine summer visits with five or six grandchildren. My grandmother said that Aunt Effie had inherited the same nomadic habits that my great-grandfather had inherited from his prairie ancestors. Aunt Effie's husband—Uncle Tinney, a confidence man on the run from the law most of the time—further encouraged her to drift. Every few months they had to move in the middle of the night, when Uncle Tinney got word that the sheriff knew about a still in the woods behind the house. Everyone said that Uncle Tinney threw good socials. Cooked deer and pork over open pits all night, sliced the tender meat into greasy light-bread sandwiches, and roasted ears of fresh corn. He made a healthy living charging his guests for every bite they ate and every drop they drank. There was nowhere else for country folk to go. So, they ate, drank, and danced the night away at Uncle Tinney's to the music of guitar-picking Cousin Hudge—when he wasn't traveling in minstrels or on the road playing in a medicine show.

During those few days of my grandmother's absence, no one came to our house to mooch. Without that protective crowd of relatives around her, my beautiful and tender-hearted mother walked through life envisioning the gruesome. Allowing her imagination to come alive and invade her mind, she got up all through the night, turning on lights to check windows and doors, making sure they were still latched and we were still shielded from potential danger. Her security devices served as the psychological barrier she had been unable to construct between Johnny and his illness, a situation for which she could devise no protection. Trying hard to become a modern woman, my mother did not honor the old prairie ways of my great-grandfather. But I wondered if secretly she ever prayed for my brother's release from his pain in this world. I never could ask, though. That was her private business. I had no right to intrude.

My Grandmother's Sit=In

My grandmother's return cooled my anxieties, and I was relieved to become her traveling companion again. The last place I wanted to go, however, was a hospital—especially *that* hospital. Practically everyone I knew who had died—except my great-grandfather, who had refused to go—had died in the Navasota hospital.

"Why did we have to come here?" I asked.

"Sometimes people have to do things that help them get over their fears," she said, straightening my coat collar. "I don't want you growing up superstitious and afraid of your own shadow. Superstition, magic, and luck destroyed your prairie people and your slave people."

"Bigmama, please, don't make me see Cousin Ready Mae."

Aunt Effie's daughter, Ready Mae, had lost control of her car and run into a neighbor's porch. I'd overheard my mother, who had visited Ready Mae a few days before, telling my grandmother that Ready Mae was bandaged from head to foot and there were tubes going everywhere. I dreaded seeing that. My grandmother asked my mother if Ready Mae's eyes looked sealed. My mother said yes. My grandmother wanted to know if Ready Mae's body had swelled. My mother said yes. My grandmother inquired about Ready Mae's ability to breathe for herself. My mother said no. What a shame, they agreed, because Ready Mae had a husband and a house full of small children expecting her to get well one day and come home.

"Ready Mae is my niece and she's dying," Bigmama said to me calmly. "I'm going to pay my respects. I want you to go, too. It may help you get over treating my father the way you did."

Ouch! Her words stung. We got out of the car. Uncle George told Bigmama he'd be back for us later and drove away. I followed my grandmother up the sidewalk. She pushed the door open, and we went into the hospital. Disinfectant, rubbing alcohol, and flowers hit my nostrils, reminding me of another place I hated just as much—a funeral home.

In the lobby, a couple of nurses behind the front desk ignored my grandmother's inquiry while they helped others who arrived after we did. My grandmother did not persist. Although I knew her temper to be short and hot, she never displayed a lack of restraint. Burning up inside, she walked away from the desk, stopped in front of a row of wooden benches and looked up at the hand-painted sign that read, "Colored." Like a smoking gun, she stood there staring at the sign; studying it. That was curious to me. She knew how to read. Why was she staring at the word, *colored,* like she'd never seen it before? After all, *colored* and *white only* were the first words southerners learned to read and the only words all illiterate southerners recognized.

I'd been reading *colored* since I was three. When Bigmama taught me to recognize the word, I was so young I don't remember yet having seen my own reflection in a mirror. When I was drawing on the floor one day, she knelt, picked up a crayon, and, on a piece of my paper, wrote a word in large black letters. She called out each letter as if trying to make me aware of our vulgar circumstance without soiling me in the process.

"I'm sorry I have to teach you this ugly word, *colored,*" she said. "I don't want to! I have to! I wish I didn't! But if I don't make you understand, you'll have one hurt after another all of your life, or you'll go out and get yourself killed."

I stared at the letters she wrote.

"This is where we have to sit when we go out, Baby."

I was too young to understand.

"This word is wrapped in a hundred years of dirty politics."

I didn't understand that, either.

"It's their way of trying to keep you in a low place and make you feel like dirt, so you'll stay down on the ground." She dropped the crayon. "But you just remember, Baby, you're not dirt, no matter where they make you sit. Your place is as high up as you push it."

I stared at the letters and never forgot their arrangement.

Bigmama turned from the scribbled hospital sign that read, "Colored," and walked to the spacious other side of the waiting area. What was she doing? Without so much as a glance up at the "White Only" sign, she eased herself down into an upholstered chair. Throat clearing did not disturb her composure and quiet dignity. She crossed one slender ankle in front of the other and tucked her feet under the chair so only the toes of her black leather shoes peeked out. Her white-gloved hands removed a silk floral scarf from her head, which she folded neatly and placed in her black leather purse. The heavy gold clasp aroused an echo in the hushed room. Looking my way, she patted a chair beside her. Timidly, I walked over, sat down, and stared at her stony expression, looking straight ahead.

My grandmother was born in 1890 and—like my mother, who was born in 1928, and me, born in 1949—had known only segregation. After sixty-five years of compliance, my grandmother had had enough. "*Brown v. the Board of Education of Topeka, Kansas,* says I can sit where I want," she said, hardly opening the razor-thin lips that reminded me of the old man. "The Supreme Court ruled it. I want to know if it's true." She explained that a little girl named Linda Brown had sued the school district for forcing her to attend inferior schools. Because she was not a white student, the law disqualified her from attending the district's better schools, limiting her access to an education equal to the one the district provided for white students.

"If that little girl can go all the way to Washington, D.C., and do all of that," Bigmama said, "then, surely, an old woman won't let a Black Code keep her from taking a comfortable chair. Black Codes have been on the books since they brought slaves to this country," she said. "And those codes are not just for Negroes. The codes keep black folk, black Mexicans, and prairie Indians in their place. Don't expect those laws to disappear overnight. New laws won't affect where you go to school or anything else you do for a very long time. Changes like that could take forever."

Afraid that my grandmother and I would be arrested or worse, my blood ran cold sitting under that "White Only" sign. I was proud and ashamed at the same time but too terrified to look up and see other people watching us. "I was about your age when the Supreme Court used the railroad to legalize what they called 'separate but equal,'" Bigmama said. "It was 1896. *Plessy v. Ferguson* made things separate, but it sure didn't make them equal."

Bigmama shifted in her chair and looked at me, whispering, "All Mr. Plessy wanted was a first-class train ticket. Well, he could spend first-class money on a first-class ticket, but Jim Crow said he couldn't put his black behind in a first-class seat."

"Who's Jim Crow?"

"A minstrel-show figure with a shiny black painted face and big white lips," she said, glancing up at the sign. "Two nations under God, one 'white only' and the other one 'colored.' They wrote laws to keep us from using their restrooms, drinking from their water fountains, trying on clothes in a store, eating with them, going to school with them, marrying them, and being buried under the same dirt with them."

"Was Jim Crow before or after the South lost their war?" I asked softly, hardly breathing.

"The North may have won the Civil War in the history books, but the South didn't lose," whispered Bigmama, smiling with a frown between her eyes as she often did. "The North gave the South everything the South was fighting to keep; because the North, the South, the West, and the East all wanted the same thing—us in a low place."

My grandmother stood up, smoothed her coat, and politely nodded to the other stunned hospital guests. "I'm going now," she said. "I never stay long where I'm not wanted. You don't have to go in Ready Mae's room if you don't want to. You can stay here."

I sprang out of that chair, not sure where I would feel more out of place—seeing Cousin Ready Mae in her condition or sitting alone under a sign that read, "White Only."

The Tutu

Bigmama and I met Uncle George at the end of our grassless yard. He rolled down the car windows and closed me and a bag of stiff pink tutu lace into the back seat. Bigmama got in the front with him, and we were off to Iola to see Aunt Celia, who had agreed to make my dance costume for the Spring Festival.

Few Candy Hill people knew what a tutu was before Mrs. Lyles, the ballet instructor—whose husband was a graduate student at Texas A&M—came to the neighborhood soliciting students. When Mrs. Lyles gave each mother a fuzzy purple copy of the outfit sketched on white typing paper, she said she wanted the tutus to be perfect replicas of the ones professional ballerinas wore. My grandmother looked at the rough sketch and declined making the tutu, mumbling something about failing eyesight. Mrs. Rouse, who lived down Dansby Street from us, looked at the drawing of the tutu and claimed she was too busy making prom dresses for Kemp High girls. Without seeing the copy first, Aunt Celia said she'd give it a try. But after seeing the rough sketch and realizing there was no pattern, Aunt Celia dropped out of contention along with the other seamstresses. "I don't have time," she said. "I had to take on extra work this month."

My mother, who didn't sew at all, hotly accused all of the seamstresses of being afraid of trying to make the strange little garment. "Excuses!" My mother's temper wasn't as short and hot as my grandmother's, but I knew she was boiling. "I'm sick and tired of backward-thinking people," she said. "You try and try to do something different to elevate your child, and you can't get any cooperation even from the child! Everybody whining some excuse."

I was glad Aunt Celia didn't want to make my tutu. I didn't want to be in the festival or any of the other of my mother's activities. As if regular elementary schoolwork wasn't enough, she enrolled me in piano lessons and signed me up for dancing lessons. Confident that we couldn't afford the dance lessons, I convinced myself that I wouldn't have to perform. But somehow that woman scraped together the money. Maybe she took on extra work or shaved something off the budget, although nothing seemed to be missing, including a weekly dollar and a half for my one-hour piano lesson and a daily quarter for my hot-plate school lunch. She even managed to buy fresh vegetables off the back of Mr. Tommy Johnson's farm truck. For awhile we didn't buy fish from the fish man. A young neighbor, who rode a flat-bed truck to the Brazos Bottom every day to chop cotton, fished in the river a couple of hours after work and brought part of his catch to my grandmother. We teased that the boy, young enough to be her grandson, was enamored of her and used the fish to try to make an impression. My grandmother, aware of her own beauty even in her advancing years, didn't appreciate our humor, although she never refused the young man's fish.

"I don't understand why you're doing this to me," I complained to my mother about the dancing lessons. "I don't have time to play anymore. Study! Study! Study! And piano lessons! Mrs. King fussing that I don't practice enough! Mr. Pruitt telling me to work out more, tighten up my forward flips, and straighten up my handstands!"

"You don't have to understand," my mother said softly. "Understanding is my job. Your job is to do it."

One Saturday morning, my mother and I walked to Lesters' Department Store in downtown Bryan, where the salesman frowned in confusion when she told him to fit me with ballet slippers. Using our entire clothing budget, my mother bought slippers, leotards, tights, and tutu lace, which remained bagged until, one day after work, my mother grabbed the bag of lace that had traveled to and from Iola, took my hand, and walked me to Aunt Lucille's house. The screen door was unlatched. My cousins played in the yard. We walked inside. Aunt Lucille was still wearing her apron. She hadn't long ago walked home from work across town, where she—like my mother and many other Candy Hill mothers—kept other women's houses spotless and dust-free, minded babies who were not their own, and served meals to families who counted the number of times they chewed their food. I smelled cornbread baking in the oven and a pot of pinto beans mixed with chopped onions and thick red juice—a familiar sweet and peppery aroma.

"I really hate to bother you with this tutu business, Lucille," my mother said, glancing out the window at Aunt Lucille's children playing in the yard. "I know you have girls of your own to sew for. When would you have the time . . . "

"It shouldn't take more than an hour to make it," Aunt Lucille reassured my mother while she studied the drawing. "You'll be home before dark." She sat down at her old Singer sewing machine beside the open window and surrounded herself in powder-pink tutu lace. A warm breeze swirled around her face, gently moving soft curls that had escaped her hairnet.

Aunt Lucille's mysterious knowledge took over, and the tutu began to appear like magic! My mother hovered near, hands shaping the air and firing sparks in the space between us. My imagination conjured pictures of me, draped in pink from head to toe, leaping across a big footlit stage. I didn't pretend to know the composition of the mystical light that had captured the three of us and inspired me to dance in the festival. I did know that I'd never mention that magical force to my grandmother. She'd dismiss all of the illogical rambling I'd require to explain this moment.

The steady pumping motion of Aunt Lucille's dusty shoe on the sewing-machine pedal sent the fragile pink fabric cascading onto the floor, to the rhythm of the faint machine buzz. Stopping every now and then, Aunt Lucille straightened seams, adjusted fabric, put in or removed a pin, and pulled threads. Without thinking, she seemed to know what to do. Catching a glimpse of me looking at her, she smiled and held the tutu out to me: "Come try this on."

My satisfied mother clasped her hands together, prayerfully, as Aunt Lucille's heavily veined hands skillfully fitted the gathered garment around my waist and pinned perfectly crafted parts into place without sticking me once.

Cousin Hudge, the Traveling Fiddler

Every time good fiddling came on her old 1950s battery radio, Bigmama started talking about Hudge, her first cousin on her father's side. "All of that side of my family was close to full-blood," my grandmother said, picking up an ear of corn from the stack we were shucking on the front steps.

"Full-blood what?" I picked up an ear and inspected the silk tail pouring out of the end. Worms could hide in there.

"Prairie Indian."

"What in the world is a Prairie Indian?" I peeled back the shuck and released fresh sweetness unique to young tender corn.

"That's what we called Comanches."

"Was the old man a Indian?" I whispered, hardly breathing.

"So close it'd be hard to make anything else out of him."

"Then how did an Indian end up a slave on a plantation?" I finally took a deep breath and placed the corn in the pan.

"He was born after slavery," she said, pulling a shuck off an ear and thumping away a worm. "Never lived on a plantation."

"How did his prairie people end up there?"

"Prairie people were raising lots of hell in these parts during slavery time," she said. "Folks didn't think any more of them than they did of Africans. And when traders could get away with it, they stole their babies, branded them, and sold them the same way they did Africans."

My mouth dropped open, and I started shaking at the thought of a hot iron on baby skin.

"After slavery, lots more Indians hid out and mixed with Africans to keep from being put in the pen or killed," she said. "Cut off their hair and they blended right in. Town folk around Anderson paid little attention to anybody who wasn't white. They couldn't tell one kind from another kind, or full-bloods from half-breeds."

"Did your father give you the Indian name that Uncle George calls you?" I stared at her for a long time, while she decided not to tell me anything more. How well I knew that look.

"We're going to leave this talk alone, now." She seemed to snap back from somewhere far away. "You don't need to know that old slaverytime prairie business. I didn't teach it to my children, and I'm not telling you. The old way is gone. Knowing about it can't help you in this world."

"But Bigmama . . . "

"Folks scared of the word *Comanche,* gal!" she scolded. "They hate anybody they believe got one drop of that blood. Safer to be African than Comanche!" I shivered. "Now, let it rest!"

"That's why you hate it when Uncle George call you by your other name," I whispered.

Subsiding into aloofness, she seemed to forget I was even there. She wouldn't have been more alone on a mountaintop with the wind. I didn't mind allowing her to escape. I'd found myself doing the same thing when something annoyed or bored me.

"Hudge's fiddling was so sweet, it made old people cry, babies laugh, and dogs howl like they do when a train is passing or there's a full moon," she said, listening to the radio and swaying back and forth. She placed another clean ear in the stack of shucked corn. "Just the thought of his fingers running up and down the strings brings back every good feeling and every sad one, too, I ever felt in my life."

Cousin Hudge was born around the turn of the century in Grimes County, near Anderson, Texas. A musical genius, he never had a music lesson or a math lesson or a reading lesson or any other kind of lesson. My grandmother said he came into the world with common sense, a mind for trickery, and hands that hated dirt. So he started picking up music and manners early to avoid working in the cotton field on the plantation where his branch of the family lived well after the emancipation of slaves.

"Somebody in the big house threw an old fiddle in the trash barrel to be burned with the garbage," Bigmama said. "Hudge grabbed that hot rim, pulled the barrel over on him, searched through the flames and found that old fiddle before the fire popped the first string."

Before long, Cousin Hudge was playing spirituals and shouts he heard the elders singing at the praise house, a worship hut developed during slavery and still used by former slaves who lived on plantations. By the time Hudge was twelve, he was composing original melodies and lyrics that incorporated spirituals and work-song variations. At thirteen, Cousin Hudge took that old half-burned-up fiddle and hopped a freight train to New Orleans, where he was hired to fiddle for a two-bit road show that traveled to one-horse towns around Louisiana. Traveling, Cousin Hudge picked up a guitar, which everyone back in those days called a box, and started playing it with the same skill he applied to the fiddle.

"I believe Hudge could play anything with strings on it if he tried it once," Bigmama said. "He picked up a man's banjo one time and strummed that thing like it was part of his own body."

"Where'd you learn to play that, Hudge?" everyone asked.

"Never had my hands on one of these before," he told them, admiring the instrument. "Seen a fellow playing one down in St. Louis. Feels pretty good."

"Hudge loved the guitar best of all," my grandmother said. "The songs he could pluck on the box were so much sadder than the fiddling or banjo strumming. All the folks 'round home loved his box playing best. I guess the sad box music came closest to the way we all really felt."

A traveling medicine man heard Cousin Hudge singing and playing and convinced him to join his show and travel by wagon to faraway places out west. Cousin Hudge said his best gig was fiddling with a white minstrel group he met out west. They played across the country in big concert theaters, show rooms, and vaudeville.

"Hudge never made any more money on the road than it took to eat and stay clean and pressed," Bigmama said. "He loved good clothes, sharp creases in his pants, and sweet-smelling cologne. Then, he couldn't afford a stamp to put on a letter if he knew how to write one. Rode the train in the baggage car, slept in the corner on hotel floors, and ate with bums and stray dogs from California to New York, while the rest of the minstrels had real beds in their own rooms and ate fancy food in dining cars."

Cousin Hudge said that one night after a show, the minstrel guys told him they didn't need him anymore. They let him go while they were playing somewhere up north. The music and movements lost their luster without him. Hoping they'd take him back, Cousin Hudge hung around the stage door for a few nights after his dismissal. But audiences not accustomed to his authentic brand of art had no way of knowing those minstrel shows were cheating them of their ticket money. The group made more money imitating Cousin Hudge's music and copying his dance steps than they ever had made playing and dancing to their own music. They never took him back. It was time to move on.

"City-slicking show people copied what they could of Hudge's music, wrote it down on paper, and signed their names to it," Bigmama said. "Then it belonged to them. They believed they'd learned all of Hudge's tunes and caught onto all his steps. But they were wrong, because every time Hudge picked up a box or a fiddle, some new sound came straight from his heart and charged up his fingers. And all the minstrels had was the little bit they were able to monkey."

Cousin Hudge said snow was on the ground when he hopped a freight train home. "I always wanted to jump a ride on a freight train." Bigmama's voice trailed off and her eyes followed. I tried to go along with her fantasy, but, as hard as I imagined, I couldn't see my grandmother's stockinged legs dangling from the open door of a moving boxcar.

"We knew Hudge was back," Bigmama whispered. "Coming through the woods, fingers running up and down the fiddle strings so fast you couldn't see them, long hair blowing in the wind. Everybody around Anderson was glad for Hudge to be off the road for a spell. We sat for hours in some kind of a trance listening to Hudge pick and fiddle us to places we'd never been."

The Case of the Missing Broccoli

"Where are the tops of the broccoli, Tony?" I asked, browsing the smelly vegetable bin examining headless stems. I looked up at Tony, the storekeeper. He owned the grocery store attached to a beer tavern at the corner of Bradley and Pierce, now East Martin Luther King Street.

"You know? The little knotty green flowers?" I asked. "What'd you do with them, Tony?"

"Gal, that ain't broccoli, and anyhow you ain't never seen none!" he shouted. "What you know about broccoli? Ever ate it? Ever seen it on Candy Hill? Ever been somewhere to see it?"

No, no, and no, I thought.

Our neighbor, Mr. Nate, grew nearly every kind of vegetable there was, but he didn't grow broccoli. Farmers drove their trucks through

the neighborhood every week selling seasonal produce such as tomatoes, greens, peas, beans, potatoes, carrots, beets, yellow squash, and
some fruits. None of them offered broccoli. And our school menu
never included broccoli. I went to the flour aisle, picked up a small
bag, and carried it to the counter.

"That all you want?" he asked, putting the flour in a brown paper
sack. Without a word, I put the money on the counter. I was furious
with Tony; so furious I couldn't see while I waited for the change
and left.

Just because I was a poor little girl and living on Candy Hill, that
lard-bellied man with grimy hands and a dirty apron thought I didn't
know my vegetables. I could name any vegetable, including any in his
store, even rotten ones covered with flies, oozing worms, and dete-
riorated beyond most people's recognition.

On my way home from the store, all I saw was red—and not red
gravel I kicked out of my way. Red anger! A playmate called my name,
wanting to play. I threw up my hand and kept stomping toward our
house, trying to think of a way to prove to that old crook—who made
all of his money peddling beer, snuff, and cigarettes to Candy Hill
adults; and candy, cookies, and potato chips to Candy Hill kids—that
I knew broccoli, even if he cut off the blossoms. Our front door
slammed behind me. In the kitchen, I handed my grandmother a
brown paper sack and her change.

"What's wrong?" she asked.

"I'm mad."

"Look like a bee went up your nose." Unconcerned, she opened
the flour, went to the stove, and dusted some of the white powder
over meat in the frying pan.

I stomped off to the living room. As I left the kitchen, I heard the
loud sizzle of the hot mixture when she added water and began stirring. The aroma, laced with onion and garlic, followed me into the
living room. Under a corner table, my mother kept a stack of old
magazines—*McCall's, Good Housekeeping,* and such. I pulled out all

of them and searched them frantically one by one until I found a picture of broccoli.

"Yes!" I shouted, running into the kitchen to show the picture to my grandmother. "Tony's down there selling broccoli stems a nickel apiece."

"You need to call him Mr. Tony," she said.

"'Cause he's white?"

"'Cause he's old enough to be your grandfather," she said.

"He's calling stems something new!" I shouted. "I know Tony cut the tops off of that broccoli."

"He probably sold the tops to a fancy restaurant," my grandmother said, looking at the picture. "Broccoli is a delicacy to rich people. They pay big money for it."

"He's trying to pass off those old no-good stems as some new thing to Candy Hill people who don't know better," I yelled, hurt twice in one day by that old swindler. "And he's selling them for a nickel apiece."

"That's all right," she said calmly. "The real substance of broccoli isn't in that pretty top. It's buried deep in the sweet tender part of the stem after you peel off that tough hide."

"Tony's the one not knowing any better?" I asked, confused.

"Run back down there and get those stems," she said, handing me a nickel. "Tell him your grandmother said she'll take all the stems he's got for one nickel and don't make her have to come down to that store and get them."

2

◆

Something Out of Nothing

Iceman

Red dust from a horse-drawn wagon brimming with fresh collard greens, tomatoes, and yellow squash hadn't quite settled back to the dirt road when my grandmother called out our front door to me, "Wait by the ditch for Mr. Mickens. He'll be coming along any time now. Tell him I need one block."

"Yes, ma'am."

"Ask him if he has any good strong ice picks to sell."

"Yes, ma'am."

"The one I bought at the store broke after one use."

"Yes, ma'am."

"Stay out of the road!"

I glanced back at the open screen door, wondering how she could see me and I couldn't see her. But that woman could see through walls; through the back of her own head; through my skull; through time. How could she see everything? How?

That particular day of my many days of wondering was a summer evening just after my fifth birthday on July 5. Still embarrassed about thinking the Fourth of July fireworks had been in celebration of my arrival into the world, my face heated up when my teen-aged cousin Charles, who lived with us for a year, came out of the house and stood over me. "You're crazy!" he said.

"I'm not!" I yelled. "But you are; pretending to be driving a car, pretending to be going somewhere fast, pretending to be smart, pretending to be important."

"You're the one pretending," he said, laughing. "You don't look like anybody else in the family. You don't even talk like everybody else. Trying to put yourself way up there with Santa Claus. I can't believe you thought somebody cared when you were born." Laughing, he shook his head and walked down the road. "Thinking the fireworks were for you. You're crazy!"

Careful not to put my feet in the city-dug ditch filled with murky green stagnant water and crowded with hatching mosquitoes, crawfish, and baby frogs, I sat down at the end of our grassless yard and waited for the iceman. In 1954, we weren't the only family on our street or in Bryan buying a 25-pound block of ice for a quarter several times a week during the summer. Mr. Mickens had lots of customers all over Candy Hill and across town, too. A refrigerator was a luxury, just like indoor plumbing or shoes in the summertime. Our landlady, always bragging about how much meat and vegetables she had frozen, had a refrigerator and a freezer. My grandmother said the landlady could afford a freezer, the way she overcharged her renters.

"But I wouldn't eat anything out of her freezer," Bigmama told my mother one day. "Some of that food has been frozen so long it's got freezer burn. If you ask me, that greedy woman is more interested in having all that food piled up somewhere than having plenty to eat." I had wondered all day and most of that night how ice could burn something.

Refrigerators weren't possible for some Candy Hill residents who still had no electricity, either because their houses were not equipped for utility service or because they simply could not afford the deposit to have the lights turned on. When night fell on some parts of Candy Hill, it was dark enough to bump your own shadow, according to my grandmother.

One day, I was late leaving a friend's house. Her mother, squinting over hand-sewing by the window, finally surrendered to near-darkness. She struck a match and lit the lamp as I was walking to the door to leave. I'll never forget the eerie feeling of watching our tall wavy shadows rise on the walls as the oil lamp flame flickered behind soot-stained glass.

Waiting for the iceman beside the ditch, I shifted my feet in front of me and noticed how ugly they were. My grandmother said everybody had ugly feet. Wearing the sandals Aunt Ruby had given me improved the look of my feet, made them seem grownup—toes out, heels out, strap around the ankle—unlike the baby-white hightops my mother made me wear in the winter. "Hightops are good for your ankles," she said, making a little bow and patting my foot. "You may be a dancer one day." Because of her concern for my ankles, my mother had determined when I first started walking that I should wear hightop shoes. Not allowing my feet to touch the floor caused me to develop soles so sensitive I wouldn't walk barefoot; I just sat or crawled.

Observed individually, my grandmother thought, all body parts were ugly. "You ever studied an elbow?" she once inquired. "Ugliest thing you ever laid eyes on. And knees look like two old monkeys." I contracted the muscles around my knees and made them bounce up and down. Monkeys talking. I laughed at my knees, and they seemed to laugh back at me.

I heard wheels grinding gravel around the corner, but it wasn't our iceman. I waved as Mrs. Rouse passed in her 1940-something Chevy. She occasionally rented one of her bedrooms, because Candy Hill visitors were allowed no hotel or motel accommodations. I was beginning to think Mr. Mickens had forgotten us until I heard his old rusty truck grinding around the corner with a fresh load of ice weighing down the back of the truck and nearly flattening the rear tires. He must have been selling a lot of ice, because he had a truck. The previous iceman, Mr. Barrows, who had gotten old and retired from the ice business, had delivered his chilly goods in a mule-drawn wagon.

As soon as the ice truck stopped in front of our house, I ran out and stood close by the vehicle to take advantage of the air passing over the cold crystal-clear squares stacked on the back. "My grandmother wants to buy a strong ice pick."

Mr. Mickens dropped an ice pick into his utility belt and took out his large metal tongs to secure a block of ice. My grandmother met us at the door. Mr. Mickens carried the ice into the house, dripping water from the front room through my mother's bedroom and into the kitchen at the back of the house. My grandmother opened the icebox. Mr. Mickens placed the block in the bottom compartment and handed my grandmother the ice pick, which she inspected thoroughly. Satisfied, she paid him and walked him to the door.

Bigmama said you should always walk people to the door when they leave your house, to be sure they're gone. "You'd be pretty uncomfortable if you thought somebody had left, and you woke up the next morning with them still there and expecting breakfast," she said. Outside, Mr. Mickens handed me an ice chip that had broken from one of the blocks. He drove away, taking his cool air with him. I sat back down on the ground and enjoyed the last of his gift, better than ice cream from Miss Rosetta's freezer. Beer-joint noise from Tony's tavern two streets over grew louder, as Saturday night intruded on my evening. With cool water running down my arm, I listened to T-Bone Walker whine from a scratched phonograph record on the tavern jukebox about his baby leaving him and how he wanted her to come back home.

My Friend, Betsy

My mother brought home lots of magazines from the house she cleaned on Mondays and Thursdays. She said that house was her favorite, even though it had ten rooms. I couldn't imagine living in ten rooms or having a refrigerator in a kitchen that had running water in a real sink or having a television in the living room or having a living room that wasn't a bedroom, too.

My mother—chauffeured like a rich person to and from work in the back seat of the car by her employer's husband—didn't care about any of the stuff those people had. She liked the couple because they gave her old magazines and because they had shelves of books that my mother borrowed secretly and brought home to read. But, most of all, my mother liked that house because the couple's grown children and grandchildren lived in another town.

Nothing made my mother more irritable than sticky fingerprints on furniture, spills, crumbs on the floor, toys scattered around, and things knocked over. I never understood why the people my mother worked for didn't make their children pick up like my mother made me pick up. She said none of the grownups she worked for picked up behind themselves, either. "Why would they make their children pick up?" She asked her question to the air. "They don't have to pick up behind themselves as long as they have me to pick up behind them."

Before I learned to read well, my mother read aloud to me everything she brought home except for the old man's dirty novels, which she read and said she didn't like. My mother read to me about the Korean Conflict, which she said was really a war, otherwise why were people shooting each other? She insisted that a conflict was supposed to be something like a cursing match and surely no more dangerous than a fistfight. Every month, I had to sit through a session of my mother reading all the world news, including sports and reports of a cold war, which I dreaded since I hated winter. Then my mother made me recite the locations of all the countries in the news and pronounce the names of all the world leaders, except those she was unsure of. We reviewed the latest inventions and modern home appliances. And, finally, we discussed current events from around the world. Then, and only then, would my mother give me the *McCall's Magazine* to keep. I turned to the page where Betsy McCall was waiting.

"Yes! There she is," I said, hugging the magazine. So much more than merely a paper doll or something to play with, Betsy McCall was my best friend. Betsy took me skiing in the Colorado Rockies, sunbathing on a Caribbean beach, sightseeing at Buckingham Palace, walking through the ruins in Greece, and visiting polar bears at the North Pole.

I retrieved my rusty blunt scissors from the shoebox where I kept all of my Betsy paper dolls and clothes from previous issues. Carefully I clipped out Betsy and her wardrobe for the month, pressed the paper tabs over her fragile shoulders to check the fit of her flowery spring frock, and wondered what trips Betsy had in store for us this time.

My Grandmother's Pharmacy

In the 1950s, the pharmacy was as close as the nearest box of Arm and Hammer or the kitchen of our neighbor, Papa Blue. Papa Blue didn't claim to cure people or make medicine. His fame was for things that made women pretty, and he tried out every one of his concoctions first on his wife and daughters. Papa Blue and his family had the smoothest skin and the shiniest hair of any people on Candy Hill. The old man made skin and hair soap, and he never told any of the women who bought it what he put in it. And they didn't ask, because it worked.

When my grandmother first tried Papa Blue's soap, his ten-year-old daughter, Rosetta Blue, who was about my age, brought it to the house. Her face was as smooth as a dark brown stone tumbled in a stream of clear water. Rosetta Blue's long, shiny braid, a mixture of chestnut, flame, and gold—colors much lighter than her skin—was pulled back in a snow-white ribbon.

"Papa said, you don't have to pay for this bar of soap," Rosetta Blue said to my grandmother. "But when you buy the next one, Papa said, you'll have to pay double."

My grandmother would have paid triple by the time her first beauty bar was finished three months later. Her hair was two inches longer, and her skin looked ten years younger.

Wednesday Was Wash Day

I heard my grandmother humming a familiar hymn to the rhythm of her knuckles on the rubboard and the periodic splashing of sudsy laundry water over the sides of her galvanized washtub.

That must have been on a Wednesday, because, in the 1950s, on Wednesdays our Candy Hill neighborhood was decorated with colorful clothes swaying in the breeze on backyard clotheslines. No one I knew had a real washing machine, but I'd seen one in a magazine. Although I'd once heard my cousin James Arthur from Houston mention something called a "laundromat," I didn't know if such places existed in Bryan. I knew I didn't know of one on Candy Hill. And it didn't matter anyway, because most Candy Hill folks washed the old-fashioned way.

Miss Rosetta, a widow with no children at home, who lived across the street, put out a small weekly hand wash of lacy underthings, handkerchiefs, head scarves, and shiny nylon stockings. A beauty operator and owner of a small store attached to her house, Miss Rosetta had no time to wash heavy loads. She sent her sheets and towels next door to Miss Willie's laundry.

Aunt Gnat lived down the trail in back of our house. At least one hundred years old and having outlived her relatives, she was no one's aunt. Her clothesline was full of assorted rags and odd-sized garments I couldn't recognize from the distance. Across the dirt road that ran beside our house, Mrs. Hines strung her clothesline and yard fence with Mr. Hines's blue denim coveralls and white longjohns, which she threw into a big black iron pot to boil out the smell of the chickens her husband raised.

In the shadow of the house, I stood quietly out of sight. If my grandmother knew that I or anyone else was listening, the humming would stop. Never having heard her sing out loud, because she made these sounds only while doing the laundry, I wasn't sure if my

Sunny Nash at age two in a photo booth in Bryan, Texas, 1951.

grandmother really couldn't carry a tune or if she was just shy about her voice. She wrung out a dress and cotton stockings and tossed them in the rinse bucket. My blue romper she dropped into a soak bucket.

Thinking bib-front pants were for babies crawling on the floor and drooling, I hated wearing rompers. But every time I hid them, my grandmother found them and remarked that many babies were about my size and that if I didn't start eating vegetables, that's the size I'd stay. As a seven-year-old, she reminded me that I could wear clothes meant for a doll Aunt Clara sent me. People thought my mother was taking me to nursery school when she was walking me to first grade.

My grandmother slapped my blue romper onto the rubboard and began grinding out a week's worth of my sweat and the red dirt that

drifted from the dusty road running in front of our house. Eaves-
dropping on her private recital, I eased myself to the ground, rested
my back against the house, and allowed the muted tones that poured
from her throat like warm honey to comfort me.

Ribbons from the Grave

Late one evening I was walking home from Peaches and Wanda's house
near an area of Bryan known as the Graveyard Line, which adjoined
my Candy Hill neighborhood.

Because my age nestled perfectly between Peaches and Wanda's
ages—six and eight—and our mothers were friends, I was allowed to
walk home with the sisters after school some days. We secretly read
steamy stories in their mother's *True Confessions* magazines and
dreamed about moving to Houston when we grew up.

Peaches and Wanda were my best friends until we got to junior
high school and went our separate ways. That's when I met Mildred,
who most people said looked just like me. For years, I'd been mis-
taken for Mildred. And when I met her, I saw why. Trying to concoct
a blood relationship to justify our resemblance, we quizzed our parents. When we failed to discover any family ties, we became best
friends.

People living near Peaches and Wanda's Graveyard Line neighborhood were just as poor as people living on Candy Hill and those who
owned their own homes, few owned cars. Traffic there consisted of
rich people bringing domestic workers home from work. Unlike my
Houston cousins, we walked everywhere, because Bryan's first bus
service went broke and left town.

I loved going to Peaches and Wanda's house. Every room smelled
like fresh cedar clippings, pinecones, peppermint, and tea cakes, even
when the oven was cold. Religious pictures—the Lord's Supper, pray-

ing hands, and portraits of deities—adorned the living room walls. Under a sheet of clear glass on the coffee table in their living room, little children in family photographs squinted into the sun and grinned toothless smiles.

On other table surfaces in the living room, antique vases, ceramic figurines, candy bowls of sweet morsels, and tall lamps with dangling teardrops perched on white doilies. Softly patterned light spilled onto the dark brown living room rug through lace curtains draped at windows and resting on the backs of a slip-covered couch and matching chair. In other parts of the house, beds were neatly made, colorful bottles lined their mother's dresser, and no dust was allowed to accumulate.

Peaches and Wanda weren't rich. Like my mother and most other mothers I knew, their mother was inventive and accustomed to making something useful or attractive out of a scrap of nothing. Meals and wardrobes, in our house and in most of my friends' homes, called for budget-stretching planning. According to my grandmother, a ten-cent bunch of mustard greens from Mr. Tommy Johnson's vegetable truck made a perfect meal when served with a pan of hot-water cornbread cakes. "If you drink the pot liquor off the greens, you won't catch a cold," she said.

"At school they say orange juice keeps you from catching a cold," I announced to my grandmother.

"Orange juice never kept anybody from catching a cold," she scoffed. "I don't care what they say at school. Pot liquor!"

"Yes, ma'am."

I saw nothing wrong with drinking pot liquor instead of orange juice or wearing hand-me-downs instead of new clothes, as long as the hand-me-downs fit. My mother liked good clothes that no one had ever worn, though.

"Your mother was privileged," my grandmother had explained to me. "She never had to wear hand-me-downs. When she was growing up, the family still had money and property. Your mother was the youngest child in the family. What I didn't give her, her four sisters or two brothers got for her."

Every once in awhile, though, my grandmother got some great hand-me-downs from someone she knew and sneaked them into my wardrobe, hoping my mother wouldn't notice.

I could feel myself getting into trouble because it was getting late. Graveyard Line domino players already were pulling kitchen tables almost into the street for their nightly games and setting up tubs of iced beer. These friendly games drew large crowds who watched or bet on the action. If a car happened into the area, it was likely to be stared down by the crowd.

Oh, occasionally, a few hot words passed, followed by some light cursing. Once I heard someone say that a guy was pulled out of his car and slapped around for interrupting a domino game with his car horn. Surrounded by Graveyard Liners, people in cars usually lost and had to back out of narrow streets or find some way of turning the car around so they could get out of the neighborhood. Games always resumed with loud bursts of laughter and a player slamming down a bone on the table and shouting, "Twenty-five! Read 'em and weep, sucker!" The sound of a domino game traveled for blocks before being neutralized by some other neighborhood noise, like a whining jukebox at the Four Way In beer joint, a baby crying, or two snarling dogs fighting over a piece of rotten meat they'd found at someone's back door.

"Hey, little gal," a boy not much older than I was called out to me from the domino yard. "It's late. Get on home, now."

"Hey, Thomas Earl Childs," I called back. "I'm on my way home. Miss Lou Della know you up here playing dominoes?"

Glancing over my shoulder from time to time, I noticed that the sun was drifting faster behind trees and rooftops than I was walking. Knowing I'd be in trouble if the day's last light disappeared before I got home, my pace reached near running. Before long, sweat poured from my scalp. The only way I could get home on time was to take a shortcut through the cemetery, where the town's affluent deceased residents were buried. Ordinarily, I wasn't afraid to skip over the soft green lawn and traipse among headstones and grave markers. Sometimes I stopped to read names and ancient dates. Before the caretaker chased me away one day, I wandered about for more than an hour, imagining shawled ladies, linen-suited men, young boys in knee pants, and little girls with ribbons streaming from their hair.

But it was too late that day for lingering. Tall oak trees and flowering shrubs, swaying in the breeze, cast long willowy shadows across my path, where bugs in the grass appeared to be monsters. As dusk descended and night noises spooked me, friendly ghosts quickly lost their humor. Then I saw comfort—someone's mother in the distance, kneeling between graves. Probably on her way home from work, she was gathering ribbons from vases and potted plants around fresh mounds. Carefully, she spooled the ribbons around her wrist. After washing and ironing the white, pink, red and yellow silk strands, the woman would give her daughter pretty ribbons to match every outfit. Without disturbing her delicate duty, I reached the fence on the other side of the cemetery and climbed over, moments before sunset.

The Dressing Table

I stepped over the threshold into my mother's tiny bedroom, where everything had a place. Framed magazine landscapes hung on fading floral wallpaper. Pillows nestled under a shedding white chenille bedspread. Draped over open windows that formed a perpendicular angle of light in the room, sheer curtains were pulled apart with dime-store ribbons. On a bedside table, my mother conveniently had arranged a reading lamp, writing pad and pencil, old issues of *National Geographic* and *McCall's Magazine,* two paperback novels, a current calendar showing June, 1959, and a dog-eared copy of the King James

Version of the Holy Bible. My mother believed in everything having a place, and, just as strongly, she believed things should be in their places if they were not in use. Otherwise, she said, "How would you know where they are?"

A straw basket shaped like a casserole dish held scissors, needles, and thread for embroidery. In a Mason jar, she kept extra pens and pencils. In another Mason jar, she kept screwdrivers; an ashtray held screws; a shoebox kept hammer and nails.

"You can't be careless about a small house like you can a big one," she said when I ignored her organizational scheme. "The walls of a small house start to creep in on you if you don't put things away."

I stepped farther into my mother's bedroom. She was at work, having taken on another job so that payments on our recently acquired little cottage would not break our fragile budget. I felt uneasy that my grandmother might discover me disturbing my mother's things. My mother's new dressing table was laden with precious possessions—a jewelry box of rhinestone bracelets; matching earrings, precision-cut; stained-glass necklaces and other gold-dipped baubles and bangles; seldom-used perfume in colorful bottles; fire-engine-red lipstick; mother-of-pearl comb, brush, and hand mirror; an assortment of ponytail holders and decorative pins she used to sweep her hair from her face. I settled onto the smooth cushioned seat in front of the table.

We hadn't long ago moved out of the tiny rental house two houses down Dansby Street into the ever-so-slightly larger cottage on the corner. My mother had hired a carpenter to gut the structure and build new kitchen cabinets, complete with a sink and running water; and an indoor bathroom, for which she selected sky-blue fixtures. Although recycling was still as important to my mother as organization, she did replace our old icebox with a new refrigerator. The icebox was disassembled and used for parts in her other projects. "Poor people shouldn't throw away a useful thing," she'd say. "We may need it later."

Before the old rough wooden sideboard became my mother's dressing table, it sank with every rain into the dirt in the backyard of our new home. One day she cleaned the weather-worn table, knocked its legs into place, and took it into her bedroom. The table and a bench rescued from the garage waited for weeks while she embroidered a crisp white pillowcase and sheet to create a seat and matching tablecover. Pink roses and green stems swirled into lush bouquets and spilled to the hems of the floor-length bench and table skirts.

I looked into the mirror, retrieved from an old dresser whose drawers no longer fit. Though the glass had a few spots around the edges, my mother had repainted its chipped frame. Pretending to apply lipstick to my shapeless nine-year-old mouth, I didn't dare touch anything! She'd know.

At night, my mother ceremonially smoothed fluffy white cream on her satiny face. A faint smile crept across her well-shaped lips, and her almond eyes stared deep inside the mirror, where no other eyes could see. I watched her thoughtful reflection as her graceful fingers replaced the face-cream container in exactly the same ringed indentation it had left in the soft embroidered fabric of her dressing-table cover.

I touched nothing! She'd know.

Out of discarded junk, my mother had carved a new space, which she shared with no one. Needing no magazines to measure her elegant style and no 1950s blond beauty queens to confirm her sultry ebony charm, my mother created her own personal altar, dedicated perhaps to something very feminine and very private about self that I soon would have to learn.

A Very Special Delivery

I had been sitting on the bottom step of our small porch all morning listening for the sound of tires rolling over gravel. Shading my eyes from bright morning glare with my hand, I looked in one direction and then the other. I didn't know which route the delivery truck would take.

Trying to amuse myself, I dug around with my finger in the dirt by my feet and watched the bugs scamper. All the flowers in our yard had gone to seed. I didn't really understand what going to seed meant, but I knew what it looked like—plants sending up their ugliest flowers of the season and then dying.

Mr. Raper, the elderly gentleman from whom my mother purchased the cottage, had spent many hours a day digging, pruning, cultivating, and fertilizing the palatial St. Augustine lawn. After we moved in, though, children playing on the grass slowly erased any chance of even a blade growing in some areas of the yard, giving it the balding look of a mangy dog. In spring and summer, blooming plants somehow still managed to leap from every corner of the property. Shrubs laced with creamy-colored honeysuckle formed a boundary between us and the streets. They became a bit overgrown after we moved in, but before they got too high, my mother employed Cousin Roy to trim and shape the greenery.

My grandmother, unimpressed with everyone and anything they might have done, wasn't any more impressed with Cousin Roy's shrubbery trimming job than she was his guitar picking when they all lived in Iola back in the teens and twenties. "The bushes are suppose to be privacy bushes," she complained after Cousin Roy had finished one day. "Now, they're as thin as Spanish lace. Can't sit in the yard without every passing body seeing me."

In the backyard, a few trees still bore plums and peaches, but the fruit looked sickly. Worms got more pleasure from it than we did. Berries showered from the mulberry tree, creating thick purple mud. Along the fence, vines produced sweet dewberries. I loved my grandmother's dewberry cobblers, not-too-sweet purple gravy with dumplings under a crisp buttery crust. I hated dewberry cobblers that were too sweet; and I hated crunching seeds that got stuck between my teeth like eating gravel. My grandmother strained out the seeds.

I waited happily on the porch. A cool autumn breeze swept my legs. Brown leaves drifted from a tree in the yard. Then, before I saw the delivery truck, I heard it creeping up the side street just before it made the turn toward our house on the corner. My heart gave a leap so hard it disturbed my insides and momentarily made me a little sick to my stomach. The truck stopped close to the ditch. Two men wearing department store uniforms seemed to take their time getting out of the Good Year truck. One of them looked at a piece of paper on a clipboard and then at the numbers on our house. He scratched his head and finally nodded to his partner, who met him at the back of the truck and opened the heavy doors.

"This is the address," he said, opening the double doors at the back of the truck. The banging doors brought out our neighbor Miss Rosetta, who lived across the street. She thought no one could see her peeking through the screen enclosing her porch.

It was rare that a department store delivery truck came to Candy Hill in the 1950s. Most of us got everything we owned second- and third-hand, including the clothes and shoes we wore. My grandmother said even the food in the Candy Hill stores was so old that it must have been second-hand, too. One day she sent me to the store for a bag of meal. When I got back with it, she opened it to find bugs scurrying around. She took it back to the store herself, saying she wasn't going to pay for meal the weevils had used first.

"I want my money back!" she had yelled at the storekeeper.

"No," he said, "you bought that corn meal. I'm not giving you any money back."

"Then I'll just have to open every bag of meal on the shelf until I find one that satisfies me," she said. The storekeeper refunded her money.

The last delivery truck I'd seen in our part of town was one whose driver had taken a wrong turn and fumbled around Candy Hill's awkward layout until he found his way out. In our neighborhoods, getting lost was easy if you didn't know your way around. Half the streets didn't have signs showing their names, and many weren't streets at all, just footpaths ending at someone's front door. Some looked like cattle trails.

My grandmother said city planners deliberately laid our streets out inconveniently. "They'll build a road in a circle or just let it run out in a field or put a fence up at the end of it over in this part of town, just to keep us in our place."

"They don't care," my mother would answer.

"Oh, yeah, they care," my grandmother said. "They want to make it hard for us to get into the areas where they have to go home at night."

"Nobody cares where they go at night," my mother said.

"They don't know that," my grandmother said. "They're scared that we are as mad at them as they would be if somebody treated them as bad as they treat us."

As the delivery men went about their business, people from blocks away had followed the Good Year truck to see where it was bound and what new thing it brought. Neighborhood kids walking past our house stopped to see. With everyone staring in amazement, the men took the large console television set out of the truck.

As poor as we were, my mother had first-class style. "I may only have one dress," she'd say, "but it's the best dress money can buy, even if they wouldn't let me try it on before I bought it."

My grandmother didn't have my mother's desire for quality cloth-ing. She either made her clothes or bought them from a door-to-door salesman. "If I had a shape like your grandmother's," my mother used to say, "I could buy clothes off the back of a truck, too. If I was built like her, I could wear a skirt that didn't have enough cloth in it or had a bad cut. That woman would look good in an old flour sack with a rope tied around her waist."

My mother was right about my grandmother's beauty, unmatched by that of any of her five daughters or numerous granddaughters. None came close. My grandmother kept her waist-length black and silver hair pulled up and back, away from high cheekbones that rose under skin about the color of a brown paper sack and smoother than silk stockings. Her deep-set gray eyes nearly hid under ample eyebrows and a spray of long black eyelashes.

"And you don't even care how pretty you are," my mother said to my grandmother. "If I had your looks, I'd go to Hollywood and be in the movies with Lena Horne."

"I had nothing to do with the way I look," my grandmother said. "So, what'd I look like trying to take credit for it?"

"You're the only woman I know with looks like yours who's not twisting around out there showing off," my mother said.

"That's what's wrong with this world," my grandmother said. "People taking credit and others being blamed for things they had nothing at all to do with." I liked my grandmother's attitude about her appearance. To me that made her even prettier. I vowed that if I ever got as pretty as she was, I'd be the same. But I've never had to worry about that.

Swinging our front door open for the delivery men, I pointed out the corner my mother had designated for the television set. The men set it down. My grandmother signed the clipboard, and the men left. "I'm glad we got a television," I said.

"Where do you come up with all of this stuff?" she asked. "You've never been anywhere to see a television, and you go and ask your mama to buy one."

"Never saw a real one till now." I examined the set and ran my hand over it. "Just saw a picture of one in a magazine."

"Even the folks your mama works for don't have televisions, yet," she said disapprovingly. "Don't try to turn it on."

"A television can show funnies," I explained, not touching the knobs. "Only the pictures move. They call them cartoons."

"Everybody's talking about getting one," my grandmother said. "Nobody knows how the blasted thing's supposed to work!"

"I'm sure glad we have a television," I said, smiling.

"And nobody know how to fix the blasted thing if it breaks," she said, shaking her head and walking away.

After my grandmother told me not to touch the television, I sat in front of the blank screen. When my mother got home from work, she tuned in foggy reception from KCEN in Temple, nearly a hundred miles to the north. Later that night, after I'd gone to bed, my mother and grandmother watched a movie on KTRK in Houston, a hundred miles to the south.

The Piano Lesson

When I was nine, my mother married my father. He moved into our cottage and helped finance the addition of two rooms. Finally we had a little extra money for things like new coats, piano lessons, and, occasionally on Saturday nights, Dairy Queen hamburgers.

I hurried home from my piano teacher's house one cool evening, feeling pretty proud of myself. Mrs. King never mentioned that I had exceptional talent. That would have been a lie, because I didn't. Adequate skill is what I had. And that came from working hard and practicing every day. Mrs. King did say, however, that my hands were suited to playing piano. "Nimble." She examined my fingers. "But you will have to give up softball to protect them."

At the last recital, I had to play a piece for left hand only, because I'd jammed the middle finger of my right hand in a casual lunchtime ball game at school. My piano lessons were going well, though, and my mother said the store was delivering my piano that day.

"How was your lesson?" my grandmother asked when I ran into the house. Rushing past her through the living room, I didn't answer. She followed me, but my mind was completely occupied with the upright piano that took up most of the space in our tiny dining area at the back of the kitchen. That was the only wall in the house large enough to accommodate the huge instrument.

"Well?" my grandmother asked. "Play something."

Ignoring her, I stared at the tall piano, so much larger than it had looked in the store. I liked it, though, because it was plain; no fancy carvings of lions' heads or birds' wings emerging from the front panel or drifting down the legs. The keys were in good condition, with all of their ivories. Except for varnish over blistered wood confessing a hasty reconditioning, the piano was perfect.

"Music may be a good vocation for you," my grandmother said. "But I don't mean hanging around night spots until all hours and singing and playing the blues half-naked on a stage."

"What do you know about playing the blues?" I asked, feeling superior because I thought I knew how to do something she didn't.

My grandmother sat down and hammered out a blues as good as any I'd heard Ray Charles play on records. Without so much as a glance at me, she got up from piano—strings still humming—and never sat down to it again.

Rain Stopped Travel on Candy Hill

A dark sky poured rain into tire gullies that crisscrossed and cut into the red dirt and gravel on Dansby Street. My street. The street that passed in front of my house.

Giant drops pounded the roof and sent crystal streams rolling over raw shingle edges. Lightning sailed around in all directions, and thunder seemed to jar the floorboards under me. From the living room floor by the front door, I watched rainwater pick up debris, run into the drainage ditch, and rush off to wherever rainwater went. In 1960, there were no curbs or gutters and no plans for curbs or gutters on Dansby or any other Candy Hill street.

"Why bother calling Dansby a street?" I asked.

"I don't know," said my mother, distracted by the storm.

"It should be Dansby Road," I said. "Or Dansby Trail."

"Close the door," she said. "I hate storms."

A swift breeze swept mist over my face. "I love storms," I said. My rain-blurred picture, framed by our open living room doorway, was interrupted only by a muddy Dansby Street, which resembled Mr. Hines's rain-soaked, freshly-turned garden dirt. On rainy days, drivers who knew better usually avoided Candy Hill's network of wagon trails, overgrown alleys, and narrow footpaths. One driver, however, had braved Dansby Street earlier that day, only to slide into the ditch. The engine roared and the tires spun deeper into the muck, until smoke rose from his hood. The frustrated driver shook his head, yelled a few profanities descriptive of his knee-deep-in-muck predicament, and walked away, trying to keep the mud from pulling off his shoes.

"Why bother calling Dansby a street?" I asked again.

"I told you I don't know!" The storm was getting to her. "And I told you to close that door!"

"When will Dansby be a cement street?" I asked.

"Your father has been asking the folks downtown the same question," she said, annoyed because I made no motion to close the door. "They say they'll fix Dansby Street if the people on Dansby Street pay for it. Now close the door!"

The storm was about to end anyway. The aroma of wet dirt drifting through the open door lured me onto the porch, where cool dampness surrounded and caressed me. I closed the door behind me. Every now and then, radiance flashed in a far corner of the sky and distant thunder rumbled. Raindrops got farther and farther apart, until the last one fell. Like magic, the sounds of evening softly descended upon Candy Hill. Frogs croaked their out-of-tune song. Bugs and birds chirped, chewed, cooed, scratched, scraped, and screeched. Down the block, Jimmy Reed whined a lover-done-wrong blues from the jukebox at Tony's beer tavern.

3

◆

Summer Days

Kissed by the Sun

The summer of 1960, before I turned eleven years old, seemed much hotter than any summer in my memory. That was a few years before my mother purchased our first air conditioner, a time when no one else on Candy Hill owned an air conditioner, either. The only cool retreats during the day were lingering in front of an open refrigerator, sitting in the mist of a yard sprinkler, pretending to shop at the downtown Woolworth's, chasing down the ice cream man and hanging around his truck until he realized you had no money to buy anything, and going to the swimming pool.

Twenty-five-cent admission scraped together, blue-and-white-striped bathing suit under my shorts, and frayed pink bath towel hanging over my shoulder, I was off to Sadie Thomas Pool, where I stayed in and out of the water from one o'clock in the afternoon until after five that evening. When I got home, I was nauseous and had a terrible headache. My skin and scalp were tender to the touch. Scolding me for staying out so long, my mother noticed that my eyes were swollen from chlorine water exposure. Before I went to bed, I had turned a deep, unhealthy shade of burgundy.

In the dead of dog days, Texas air was too hot and heavy to hold for any length of time in the lungs. And that night would have been particularly dreadful without the freedom to sleep with doors and windows open to encourage a modest movement of indoor air. More concerned about attracting a breeze than a thief, I abandoned my scorching bed, dropped my pillow and sheet by the open kitchen door, stretched out on the cool wood floor, and buried my face in the rough pillowcase. My nose found slightly sweet scents of dust trapped in cracks between dead planks.

I heard the blades of my grandmother's little black fan whirring in the next room. Perspiration formed in my hair and rolled down my face. Waiting for the sounds of branches to forecast a breeze, I turned my pillow to the cool dry side and listened to frogs croak. Chattering crickets gathered on the back steps, knocking their knees together to choose dance partners. Night birds harmonized with their own partners to an accompanying chorus of evening bugs. I tilted my face and felt a tickle of cool evening puffs relieving earth of the day's heat. Strings on the upright piano became haunted by the gradual change in temperature as I drifted off to sleep.

"It's time to get up," my grandmother announced the next morning. She had already begun her daily August ritual of keeping the house as cool as she could. "Sun shining in here all morning will cook us by noon." She closed the back door and pulled down the window shade to shut out blazing morning heat. Observing the angles of sunlight hitting windows at different times of the day was a critical component in her temperature control ceremony. "Have to get an early start on keeping the house cool," she said.

Steam rose from my body, damp glued wilted pajamas to my aching limbs, and sweat on my scalp stung the center part between my braids. Feeling disoriented and irritable, I peeled my eyes open and felt the wet pillow and sheet spread out beneath me on the kitchen floor, a sanctuary slightly cooler than my bed the night before.

"Heat is the reason people are so mean in the summer," my grandmother explained. "More killings in summer, because people don't have the intelligence to stay out of the sun, be still, and stay cool. In winter, people are too busy keeping warm to start as much trouble."

As I awakened more, I noticed that my arms and legs hurt to the touch and that my skin had taken on a dry, rusty appearance.

"No need dragging in hot air," she said, leaving the kitchen with her little black fan. "I'll put this in the living room window until this afternoon."

Under the protection of the front porch roof, the living room window that faced west yielded cool breezes all morning. As soon as the first afternoon light kissed the top step of the front porch, my grandmother pulled down the living room shades to keep out the sun and moved the fan to a shady location.

"It must have been ninety degrees last night," she said, returning. "Probably reach a hundred today. The sun will be dangerous. You stay in the house. You should have stayed in yesterday, too."

"Why?" I asked. She annoyed me when she started making up new laws before I was awake fully enough to defend my rights.

"You want to burn up?" she asked.

"Black people can't sunburn."

"Oh, yes, they can," she said. "I've known people much darker than you who worked all summer in the cotton field. They burned so bad their faces looked like cheap leather when they got old."

I glanced down at my arms.

"A deep burn hurts for days, and it's a real ugly sight wearing off," she said. "After they stopped hurting, they were as dried out as a lizard, and scales flaked off like a dead fish."

I stared at her in horror as she walked over to me, looked at my face, picked up my arm, and inspected it. "You're already fried! Skin is skin, no matter what color it is! You put heat to it and it burns."

And Comfort Came

The early evening suddenly had turned unusually cool. Crisp gusts were rare occurrences in a Texas summer. Accustomed to breathing air too heavy to inhale, Candy Hill folk draped their bodies over porch steps, relaxed in their yards, and allowed the day's pungent moisture to evaporate from salty skin.

"I heard the only state in this nation stickier than Texas in the summertime is Louisiana," my grandmother said from her chair a short distance from the porch. "Sure doesn't feel like Texas or Louisiana this evening."

"I'm glad nothing's on television," I said from my perch on the porch step, enjoying a breeze on my arms and legs.

"Nothing is ever on that thing I want to watch," she lied. She loved soap operas and often said it's about time we get to laugh at white folks' misery for a change. "Don't know why people make such a racket about a television. Give me a radio any day."

Television reception depended on the antenna outside our house and the lateness of the hour—after midnight, if you wanted to watch a program from Houston. Reception from Temple was acceptable most of the time, but Dallas was clear only if it was raining in Bryan. Sometimes we could make out pictures in a screen full of snow all the way from romantic New Orleans, the closest exotic spot to our awkward, small-town, urban-rural balance. In a storm, though, if lightning teased the power once, my mother shut off the set.

In the early days, visitors calculated the affluence of a neighborhood by the number of television antennas blossoming on the horizon. For a long time, ours was the only antenna on the Candy Hill horizon—a constant annoyance to my mother, who hated having people crowded into our living room. Her sensibilities were as delicate as our impeccably decorated cottage, furnished in first-class style with second-hand and makeshift pieces that she painted to match.

My mother's fingers cramped after long sessions of piecing together slipcovers and matching curtains by hand, embroidering pillow emblems and tying together colorful scraps, left over from my grandmother's quilting, to create custom throw rugs. Our porcelain and cut-glass collection may have had great value before it was chipped and ended up in a thrift shop. I remember watching my mother carefully frame groupings of magazine and calendar landscapes and arrange them precisely on the walls. Briefly, she took up watercolor and taught herself to paint nature scenes, so she'd have originals to hang.

Wondering how my mother afforded to buy all the nice things we had, everyone who visited said our house looked like pictures out of *Good Housekeeping*. As much as she wanted to discourage our neighbors from visiting, especially when they showed up at the dinner hour expecting a plate, my mother hated turning them away from watching television with us. Besides our television set, the only entertainment on the hill was beer drinking at Tony's tavern and fighting in the streets after hours.

"Nobody'll get killed tonight if it stays cool," my grandmother said.

"Good evening," said Mr. Green, passing our yard on his way home to his mother's house, where he lived.

"Good evening," said my grandmother.

"Howdy, Mr. Green," I said, thinking that for once he was sober and walking straighter than I'd seen him in awhile. The cool weather had affected him, too. The last time I got a good look at him, he'd wobbled so unsteadily he reminded me of an inexperienced stilt walker who'd sneaked into the circus act without training. Some nights, Mr. Green held lengthy conversations with the lightpost on the corner near our house, giving the neighborhood kids quite a show. One night, he chatted politely with our hedge bush, moaned once, and then landed face down in the street. I thought he was dead, but my grandmother assured me he was just drunk.

"How are you feeling this evening, Mr. Green?" I asked.

"Pretty good," he said, walking on. "Pretty good."

"I'm glad to hear it," I said. "Mr. Green—"

"All right, now," my grandmother whispered in my direction, seeming to read my mind. "Leave him alone."

"I wasn't bothering him," I defended myself.

"Don't go pushing on something when you don't know what's be-hind it," she said. I hated it when she spouted wisdom I didn't under-stand. She was always doing that and then asking if I was listening. "You hear me?" she asked.

"Yes, ma'am."

Sitting on the porch with my face tilted up to a breeze not swift enough to be wind, I watched a red glow set on Mr. Green's back as he walked home. My eyes drifted up to dying light reflecting off high gray clouds rushing into view and seconds later passing into oblivion. To my childish imagination, the rolling clouds momentarily formed the faces of some distant prairie relatives whom I'd never meet at a family reunion.

"Something stirring in the Gulf," my grandmother whispered in a voice so soft I could hardly hear her. She meant the Gulf of Mexico about 150 miles south. Although my grandmother had never seen the water, she often referred to the Gulf when skillfully explaining our local climate.

Turning her ears slightly from one side to the other, she seemed to be listening. I listened, too, but all I heard were bugs crying the way they cried every night for darkness to come, so they could do what-ever bugs do in the dark. I wondered if the same bugs came back to visit us every night. My grandmother sat very still in her chair across the yard. Her upturned face radiated the sky's changing light before her features began fading faster than the sun.

"Wind's going to change before the morning. Maybe rain."

Our neighbors' conversations and quiet laughter, floating across the yards, revealed no concern for weather. After all, nothing could stop the rain, and there was nowhere to run from the wind. Candy Hill had no storm cellars, no basements, no shelters, no sturdy walls. Because they didn't own their houses, most Candy Hill folk didn't bother repairing roofs that couldn't keep out rainwater. They'd just put out buckets and pots to catch what the roof couldn't, and they didn't worry about weather predictions. Back then, there were no television weather forecasters with meteorology degrees and fancy sports jackets standing in front of computerized, full-color, radar-driven national weather maps.

Oh, occasionally someone inquired about the swelling in Miss Katherine's arthritic knee. The woman swore that her bum knee could predict the approach and severity of almost any kind of weather disturbance. Her accuracy, however, did not go beyond cold fronts, which left her close to crippled by the time ice storms hit. Miss Katherine wasn't the only barometer in the neighborhood, though. In the old days, lots of folks claimed to be able to predict changes in the weather by aches and pains in their joints and other mysterious means that were too complicated to investigate.

A flock of birds flying in formation passed overhead.

"They know," my grandmother said, looking up.

"Know what?" I asked.

"Snakes know, too," she said. "When heavy rain is coming, snakes head for higher ground. They've got more sense than people. Snakes know."

"Snakes know what?" I asked.

"Dogs know," she said. "A dog is worth a lot more to a person than just having something to pet."

"I don't like dogs," I said.

"Old folks say having a dog is like being grounded in a thunderstorm," she said. "Instead of evil hitting you, it hits your dog."

"I'm scared of dogs," I said.

"Dogs know," she said. "Everything on God's green earth knows something about life except man."

"What about women?" I asked.

"Man means men, women, and everything in between," she said.

"Everything in between?" I asked. "What's in between?"

"Never you mind," she said. "Animals and nature tell you everything you need to know, if you watch and listen."

"Watch and listen to what?" I asked.

"Stirring in birds' wings." My grandmother looked up at another passing flock. "Comfort will pay you a visit tonight."

The sky had disappeared into utter blackness. The streetlamp on the corner flickered. Time to shine or not, the bulb failed. The yard was so dark I couldn't see my hand inches in front of my face. My grandmother's eyes cut accurately through the dark. I heard distant thunder, rolling and mumbling in their low voices in a language that most humans could not understand. But my grandmother understood. She got up from her chair, walked up the steps past me, and went into the house. A streak of lightning raced by, and thunder shook the porch. I stumbled blindly into the house behind my grandmother.

Rain fell that night on the roof of our little cottage one lonesome drop at a time. I counted the drops and thought about my friends putting pots to catch what their roofs couldn't keep out, until the trickle became a gusher rushing off our house in streams.

At bedtime, the pillow met my face like a cool cloud. My eyelids surrendered; me eyelashes lay down in repose; and, like my grandmother said it would, comfort came. Soon, I was drifting toward an aroma of fresh bread baking in an oven. I felt fallen leaves crushing under my feet. I smelled the fragrance of cedar and rose petals and felt the warmth of crackling wood. Then I arrived at a soft spring pallet, composed of all the shades of green blades under swaying branches in a glade where I lay with northern breezes kissing my face and tracing pretty pictures in my palms. And comfort reached out of the dark with a kindly hand that stroked away the pain of my life to come and wiped from my weeping eyes tears I was yet to cry. Brightening the overgrown trail I had not begun to tread, comfort gave me a reassuring smile and became my fellow traveler that cool summer night.

Footsteps in the Rain

Well, our June cool spell had ended sometime during the night, be-cause I woke up sweating. And all memory of those gentle puffs of Arctic air—the ones that had survived the trip across Texas moving toward the Gulf of Mexico—had faded while dreams still traipsed in my sleeping head. Things were back to normal. Hot! That's how Texas was supposed to be in June. Hot!

When I got up, my grandmother sent me to the store. Tony didn't have what she wanted, so I went farther, to a store not too far out of our neighborhood. The concrete steps leading up to the store burned my feet through the soles of my blue rubber thongs. I'd wanted red thongs, but so had everyone else in Bryan. Woolworth's had sold out of red ones long before Mama got there with her forty-nine cents. I didn't dare touch the hand rail and risk roasting my fingers. Heat waved from the metal Mrs. Baird's Bread bench beside the door and disappeared overhead.

The worn screen door flew open. A grimy little boy ran out with a handful of Jack cookies. I went inside the store. Damp cool met my face, feeling much like I imagined a dungeon would. The floor planks spoke a squeaky language under my feet. The storekeeper was nowhere in sight. I tiptoed over to the old-fashioned soda cooler. My heart raced as I grasped the rubber handle of the insulated lid and peeked inside. Large chunks of ice swam in dark frigid water. Assorted bottled flavors sat randomly at the bottom of the chilly holding tank. I could steal everything in the store, I thought, squinting to read the soda labels and letting the cold air refresh my steaming face.

A man's groan shocked the cooler lid from my hand. Chipped red and white paint fell from the cooler. The storekeeper sprang straight up from behind the counter like a surprised jack-in-the-box, looking directly at me while zipping his trousers.

The girl, not much older than me—ten or eleven—stood up with her hand outstretched to the storekeeper. "Give me my five dollars, man," she demanded, snapping her fingers.

"Five dollars!" he shouted. "You think I'm going to give you five dollars 'cause somebody seen us?"

"I don't need no witness to tell your wife," she said.

"You never get more than fifty cents, and you know it," said the storekeeper. "Anyhow, you didn't finish!"

I picked up the cooler lid, peered back inside, and minded my own business. On Candy Hill where I came from, folks got killed for butting into other people's situations or even looking like they were interested. The cash register made a ding-ding sound when he opened the drawer. I didn't look up.

"That's more like it," the girl said.

I glanced up from the soda cooler. The tail of her blue dress disappeared out the door. Eyeing me, the storekeeper walked to his butcher block. The cleaver stood on its blade in the wood. He began arranging discolored steaks on a display tray. I reached inside the soda cooler. Icy water deadened my fingertips. Cold pain crept up my arm. I fished out a Big Red the first time.

The lights in the store blinked.

Lightning raced around the sky.

Thunder shook the cooler lid out of my hand.

Giant splats of rain hit the sidewalk, slowly at first. Then rivers flowed past the door. Rain blew in through windows high on the front wall. The storekeeper grabbed a long pole with a hook at the end and began closing windows. Lightning sliced the sky again. Thunder shook canned vegetables and jars of fruit on the shelves. Rain poured off the gutterless building.

Convinced that my fingertips would never revive, I slung cold water from my hand. I walked to the front, pulled off the cap with a bottle opener attached to the counter and set the soda down. He winked, met me at the register, opened the drawer, and placed a five-dollar bill on the counter. I stared at the money.

"Take it, little girl," he said.

I reached for the money. He held onto it, pressing the bill to the counter with his pudgy fingers. I tried to pull the bill out without tearing it. He never gave any girl five dollars for doing nothing! Well, I wanted that five dollars! But I wasn't going to do whatever it was that girl was doing to him to get it. We struggled over the five-dollar bill. His fingertips had turned white pressing the money to the counter. I broke out in a fine sweat. Yes! I was winning. The money was in my hand. Not to be completely outdone, the storekeeper let go of the bill, grabbed my wrist, and with his other hand reached for what would one day be my breasts. My Big Red crashed on the concrete floor. I twisted away with a firm grip on the money.

"Give me back my five dollars!" he yelled, out of breath and annoyed when I stepped out of reach. "If you can't play right, get out of my store!"

I stuffed the money in my pocket and walked out.

Dinner at Aunt Shorty's

I walked home from school in a daze, with late spring rain bouncing off my head. A car passed and splashed my favorite red pleated skirt. I didn't care that my shoes were muddy, socks soaking, clothes stuck to my body, or hair plastered to my head. Nothing mattered except my train trip to Denver that June of 1961 with my grandmother to visit her daughter and son-in-law.

I had ridden a bus to Houston to visit Bigmama's son Evans and her brother Primus, but I'd never been out of Texas or on a train. Uncle Evans, formerly married to Aunt Lucille, lived in Third Ward with his second wife, whom everyone called Babe. They ran a restaurant and bar on Leeland. Uncle Primus and his wife Nona Mae, both retired schoolteachers, lived in a part of Third Ward called Sugar Hill because of the big fancy houses there. Very strict about keeping the house clean, Uncle Primus followed everyone—including Aunt Nona Mae—with a damp cloth and made me go to bed just after sundown. I preferred visiting Uncle Evans and going to the bar with him and Aunt Babe and watching their beer-guzzling regulars come in and hustle each other at the pool table. After closing, the couple let me stay up the rest of the night watching scary movies on television.

My mother decided that Third Ward was too much like Candy Hill. She said I needed to see parts of the country that were not flat and monotonous, meet people who didn't speak with a lazy flat drawl, and experience something besides a miserably hot Candy Hill or Third Ward summer. She wanted me out of Texas.

"I want you to eat in a restaurant that you don't have to enter through a back door," she said. "And see a movie you won't be forced to watch from a musty balcony."

I couldn't imagine doing those things. In Texas, they just weren't allowed. Skipping along in the rain, though, I could clearly see images of myself from the window of a fast-moving train. The real trip, of course, was better than anything I could imagine. My grandmother and I boarded the Texas Zephyr at the North Zulch train station. North Zulch, halfway between Bryan and Madisonville, wasn't much of a town. Its train station, a tiny white one-room building on the side of the track, wasn't much of a station except that it had no designated "white" and "colored" waiting areas. My grandmother led us to our seats in an integrated car. She let me have the window seat to Dallas, where we changed trains and rode overnight to Denver. Crossing big blue rivers and deep red canyons, I watched snow-capped mountains high in the distance. The seats weren't very comfortable; but, unlike Mr. Plessy all those years ago, we had the same uncomfortable seats, used the same small restroom, and ate the same cold food as everyone else on the train.

Light mountain air caressed my skin, and, from Aunt Clara and Uncle Fred's back step, I watched a shower of rain whose drops dried before they hit the ground. One evening my grandmother and I were invited to dinner with her friend, Julianne Shorty, and the elderly woman's grandniece, who was spending the summer with her. Aunt Shorty lived around the corner in an imposing house like none on Candy Hill and few in Third Ward's Sugar Hill in Houston. I was convinced that Aunt Shorty was very rich.

A tidy landscaped brick walk led to an expanse of shallow steps that framed a wraparound porch with floral-cushioned wooden furniture. A tall, oval-glassed front door opened between large columns supporting a balcony, behind whose small-paned French doors was an upstairs sitting room where Aunt Shorty had kept an office when she was—as she called herself—a frontier businesswoman, operating her own profitable restaurant for more than thirty years. Low chandelier light reflected off matching china, crystal, and flatware. More elegant than pictures in any magazine I'd ever seen, the linen tablecloth, embroidered napkins, glowing candlesticks, and fresh flowers were arranged precisely. My grandmother wasn't nearly as impressed as I. Earlier in Bigmama's life, before she lost her fortune and was forced to sell her three hundred acres of prime Grimes County farmland for a fraction of its value, she'd had money and the good life, too.

Delicious aromas came from the kitchen as Aunt Shorty brought heavy covered silver serving dishes with ease through swinging doors. I'd never seen a six-foot, two-hundred-pound woman before. Hardly saying a word to my own hostess, the niece, I was fascinated by the story Aunt Shorty told my grandmother about her life. Born in 1870-something, Aunt Shorty was the daughter of African slaves. I stared at the woman's sooty trembling lips, telling my grandmother how Black Codes and racial prejudice would have reduced her to virtual slavery, too, if she had remained down south.

"So I worked and saved and rode a dusty train from Arkansas to

Colorado," said Aunt Shorty. "Here I can live with prejudice, because the law is on my side."

After dinner, the gracious Aunt Shorty poured brandy into fancy, long-stemmed glasses for herself and my grandmother. We retired to the porch, where the niece and I played jacks. Hanging onto each word of the older women's conversation, I lost every game.

4

◆

What's Going On?

Uncle Roscoe's City

My father's brother, my Uncle Roscoe, was visiting from New York during the winter of 1959. I was ten. Uncle Roscoe had lived in New York all of his adult life, and he loved it. It showed in his face, in his way. A city man with a city man's walk and a city man's talk, Uncle Roscoe seemed to know things that we could never know in our sleepy little town of Bryan, Texas.

"There's always somebody dead on the streets of the City," said Uncle Roscoe, cutting his third piece of my mother's rich sweet-potato pie. He hadn't finished the last bite of his last slice, but he never lost the rhythm of chewing.

"That's the City," he said.

Uncle Roscoe, like all the New Yorkers I've met since, recognized only one real city in the universe—New York. When he referred to his city, he said, "the City," because, to New Yorkers, every other city on earth—or anywhere in the galaxy, for that matter—is just another town, even Houston. My mother said Houston didn't count as a real city, because all the people she knew there were the same country folk she was raised up with in Navasota, Iola, and Anderson.

Well, back then, Uncle Roscoe was the only person I knew from that far up north. True, Aunt Leslie lived in Cleveland. I wasn't sure how far up north Cleveland was, but Cleveland wasn't New York. I once knew a woman from Baltimore, but Baltimore, though closer to New York than Cleveland, wasn't New York, either.

All the family said that Aunt Clara, who lived in Denver, was from

up north; but Denver was a different north from New York. Uncle
Wince was from Oakland. He acted like he was from up north, but
Oakland was out west, and it sure wasn't New York.

"Sure is good to be home," said Uncle Roscoe.

My father, stirring restlessly in his easy chair across the room, was
waiting for Uncle Roscoe to finish eating and sipping, so they could
go out to the family farm.

I watched Uncle Roscoe pick up his coffee cup and swallow his coffee
loudly. "I need these few peaceful days down here where I know people
are not trying to kill me," he said.

"Why do you stay there, then?" I asked.

"Because I love the City," he answered proudly.

"I don't know why anybody would want to live in a place like that,"
my father interrupted gruffly. "No fresh air to breathe. Nothing but
concrete everywhere you look."

"Wouldn't live anywhere but the City," said Uncle Roscoe. "Good
jobs in the City."

"Wouldn't want one of them," said my father.

"In the City, nobody pushes me to the back of the bus like they
push y'all around down here," Uncle Roscoe said.

"Give me the country," my father said. "I know where I stand. Nobody grinning in my face and stabbing me in my back."

"No," said Uncle Roscoe, laughing. "They just stand there looking
you right in the eyes as mean as they want to and stab you in the front."

"You're right about that," my father agreed.

I joined in their hearty men's laughter. Hearty laughter isn't what
brought my mother back into the kitchen. Disinterested in these dis-
cussions, she was doing something at the stove. I sat at the table staring
at Uncle Roscoe and wishing he'd offer to take me back to Brooklyn
for a visit. Wondering how far that was from Broadway, I imagined
the excitement of New York as Uncle Roscoe described the sounds.

Car horns!

Sirens!

Police whistles!

People yelling!

"I need these few days of rest from the City every year, though," said Uncle Roscoe, gulping down the last of his coffee. My mother poured him another cup.

"People from other towns, especially little towns like Bryan, can't even dream what it's like living in the biggest, most dangerous city in the United States of America; where you're alive one moment and dead the next," said Uncle Roscoe, heaping in lots of sugar. I studied the snow-white granules dissolving.

My mother, taking another pie out of the oven, said we needed more ice cream for later on that night while we watched television. Uncle Roscoe volunteered to walk to the store before it closed and get whatever flavor I wanted, if I accompanied him.

"People don't let their little girls go to the store by themselves this late in the City," said Uncle Roscoe. "Something bad for them to see is always happening out there."

We bundled up in coats and hats and walked along the gravel road to the store. On the way, we passed two men in the middle of the street in deep conversation. They were a father and his grown son who lived together in a little unpainted wooden shack around the corner from us. Theirs was one of the last outhouses in the neighborhood. I didn't know the men well, but I'd seen them going in and out of Tony's beer joint together. As a matter of fact, I never saw one without the other. Although their voices were not raised, I sensed tension between them.

"Sure is peaceful and quiet around here," said Uncle Roscoe, not paying attention to the men. His ears were conditioned only to urban noise.

"One day, I'm going to New York," I said.

"You have to be careful in the City," he said. "Things happen fast in the streets."

Uncle Roscoe and I walked past Tony's tavern, lively with friendly beer drinkers yelling and cursing at each other. The strong odor of

urine and stale cigarette butts followed us to the front of Tony's building, where the door opened into his dingy grocery store. We went into
the cold, dark hole. Grit crunched on the concrete floor under our
shoes. The smell of a fire burning in a kerosene heater hit my nose. At
the ice cream freezer, I searched for a carton that wasn't dirty, dam-
aged, or refrozen.

"Don't hold that freezer open so long," Tony yelled.

"I'm trying to find something worth paying money for," I said, taking a box of ice cream to the counter.

"That all?" Tony asked, rolling his eyes at me and placing the ice
cream in a sack.

Uncle Roscoe nodded and paid. I took the sack and led the way
out. A noisy crowd had gathered in the street around a mound of what
looked like rumpled clothes. Uncle Roscoe and I pushed our way
through the shocked crowd. I caught a glimpse of the son lying bleed-
ing in the road. His father stood nearby, a gun dangling at his side.
Horrified, my Uncle Roscoe gasped, grabbed my hand, and dragged
me toward home. I felt sorry for Uncle Roscoe, thinking he was safe.
After all, this wasn't the City.

Long=Distance Theft

Everyone on our street had lived in the Candy Hill neighborhood for
so many years that we knew each other's full names, children's names,
all of each other's relatives, regular schedules, wardrobes, and what
was for dinner.

No stranger came to our part of town and stayed for any length of
time unnoticed. Although Candy Hill experienced violent crimes of
passion and substance abuse in the 1950s, knowing our neighbors
worked as a home security system, and the high level of trust kept
burglary in check. We didn't lock our doors. Someone was always

wandering innocently into someone else's house, looking at photographs and examining whatnots and doodads, without a notion of taking anything. One day my grandmother came in from hanging laundry to find a neighbor sitting in our living room watching *Search for Tomorrow* on television.

Times changed.

"Hook the screen door," my grandmother said, eyes sad, like we'd lost something important.

"Why?" I was curious. Our house and other houses I regularly visited had few items of much real value.

"Because someone walked into Mary's house while she was sleeping one night last month," my grandmother said.

"Last month? And you're just now telling me?" I asked. "Did they hurt her?" I was alarmed. Miss Mary was a big woman but old enough that she might not be able to defend herself.

"No."

"Did they steal anything?"

"No," my grandmother said. "They used her telephone."

Almost everyone with an emergency had used Miss Mary's telephone. I didn't understand why someone using her phone made us have to lock our doors, any more than I understood how the dull black instrument captured voices through a frayed cord from a hole in the wall. Even though I was only eleven years old in 1960, I did understand the threat of a stranger sneaking into the house. And I didn't like the idea.

"Mary's long-distance charge was over a hundred dollars," my grandmother said. "And whoever did it made a sandwich, too."

The time had come that we had to start latching the screens at night and even during the daytime when we were sitting in the living room.

Cousin Jimmy's News

Jimmy's rusty bicycle—wheels still spinning—lay in our grassless yard under the hackberry tree. Warm air from the open window beside my cot grazed my six-year-old face. After Jimmy's awkward teen-age feet hit our rickety steps, he didn't knock; just stood out there with his head hanging down like it was attached with a piece of rubber. We were still in bed that Saturday morning in August, 1955.

As quietly as a cat, my grandmother sprang from her bed across from my cot in the living room where we both slept. Her long black hair, usually kept in a bun, had fallen during the night and was draped over one shoulder. Wearing a snowy cotton nightgown with ruffles just above her smooth white soles, she stepped to the door, which we and no one else in our Candy Hill neighborhood closed in summer. At night, from blocks away, the whine of a jukebox at a nearby beer tavern and the late-night commotion of drunken patrons traveled through our open doors and windows.

My grandmother stared at Jimmy through the screen, knowing, even without knowing what, that something was seriously wrong with him. Without a word, her slender fingers fiddled with the latch on the uneven frame and pushed the sagging door open. Eyes heavy from crying, Jimmy fell into the room with a moan. His limp body slumped on bent knees against the wall beside the door.

Moving in close, my grandmother's knowing eyes searched Jimmy's. "What's wrong?" she whispered. "Is Sister Parnell sick?" Sister Parnell was Jimmy's mother, my grandmother's first cousin. They were close.

"No, ma'am," he sobbed. "Mama's fine."

"Your daddy sick?" she asked.

"No, ma'am."

"Then what is it, Jimmy?" she asked.

Jimmy's head hung low between shaking shoulders and moved

slowly from side to side. Tears dropped from his eyes, pounding our uncovered wooden floor, and splattering on planks of varying shades of brown. I'd never seen Jimmy cry. To me, he was too big and strong and smart to cry. And without even knowing what was wrong with him, I felt like crying, too.

I eased back into the hot spot on my cot, thinking of everything to keep from thinking of anything so sad that it would make Jimmy cry. I stared at water stains on the ceiling around the plain single bulb fixture, revealing that a roof had failed during the last storm. My eyes followed the fading stripes down the wall to a crack in the corner, where sunlight shimmered into the room. I held my finger in the path of the light, imagining a diamond sparkling there, and wondered if bugs came in through that hole at night.

My mind deliberately filled up with unrelated sounds. A horse-drawn wagon kicking up gravel as the fish man yelled, "Catfish! Buffalo! Fresh perch!" Patch farmers yelling, "Watermelons, collard greens, sweet potatoes!" The clothes salesman's high, shrill, whining voice, trying to convince Candy Hill ladies to buy dreadfully unstylish dresses, cotton stockings, and girdles from the trunk of his car. My mind desperately played all the sounds of people selling cloth by the bolt, shoes, insurance, jewelry, spices, wild meat, and whatever else could be grown in a garden, caught from the river, shot in the woods, rescued from someone's garbage, or stolen from a neighbor. I heard Mr. Mickens's feet dragging across our floor when he brought a clear block of ice to our ice box. But melting drops from Mr. Mickens's ice jolted me back into our living room, where Jimmy stood crying.

"What's wrong, Jimmy?" my grandmother asked again.

"Lucy is dead!" Jimmy cried, gasping for breath.

Wide-eyed horror surrounded poor Jimmy. Hot candle wax dripping onto my heart couldn't have sent sharper pains through me than Jimmy's words. Unable to speak, I sat up clutching my chest through my nightshirt. My grandmother sucked in some needed air and stumbled backward! I expected her to keel over dead from the wound of Jimmy's words, but she landed, sitting bone straight, on her bed. "No," she uttered. "No, Jimmy."

"Yes, Mama Edna," he sobbed. "She's dead!"

I covered my ears with my hands and started humming "Twinkle, Twinkle, Little Star." I felt my face gradually become distorted and heat up with tears. The rest of my body became so tight with agony, I thought I'd burst. Lucy couldn't be dead! Lucy was only twenty-something! Lucy was too young to be dead! Lucy didn't have her children yet! Lucy was too beautiful to be dead, with her pearl-necklace smile, smooth dark chocolate skin, long shiny black braid, and perfect Coke-bottle shape. Jimmy had to be wrong, I thought, shaking my head violently and knowing all the time that he was right. But I had seen Lucy yesterday walking home from the store. She had waved to me. I had waved back. Lucy couldn't be dead! Jimmy was wrong. But why would he make up such a terrible story?

"What happened?" my grandmother whispered.

Jimmy's deep brown unblinking eyes stared at my grandmother like he no longer recognized her.

"Who did this?" she demanded.

Jimmy said that the night before, Lucy had been at the tavern with her jealous boyfriend, a brute with a reputation for beating up women. He'd already spent eighteen months in prison for killing another Candy Hill woman who had a little baby. Because a stranger had whistled at Lucy from a passing car, he beat her with a heavy chain designed for towing disabled vehicles.

"I'm going to go out and do something real bad," said Jimmy.

"What good would that do you?" my grandmother pleaded.

"I want them to put me in there with him," Jimmy said, "so I can kill him like he killed Lucy!"

My world went silent. All I could hear was the sound of blood rushing around and pounding on the inside of my head, getting louder and louder. I was terrified of losing Jimmy, too. But worse, if beautiful, smart, nice Lucy could get killed on the streets of Candy Hill, the same thing could happen to me.

Shooting Without a Gun

"Damn that Brazell," she mumbled. "Can't understand why he killed our little Lucy."

I couldn't believe I heard my grandmother say a curse word.

"Damn him!" she said again.

Brazell wasn't the only killer I knew.

My grandmother had two nephews who were killers. But they didn't kill for fun, they killed for money. Spending most of their time running from the law, the men didn't visit the family much anymore. Like Cousin Hudge, they spent a lot of time jumping trains from city to city. But unlike Cousin Hudge, they were moving around making trouble, not music. Although I had trouble with the concept of one person killing another person, I understood my killer cousins better than I could understand Brazell beating Lucy to death with a car chain. To my killer cousins, it was business—nothing personal. But Brazell had deceived Lucy into loving him. You couldn't get more personal than that.

"Damn Brazell!" my grandmother said again.

I wanted to kill Brazell when he got out of jail, if only I could get to him before Jimmy and the rest of the Parnell brothers got to him or before my grandmother did the job herself.

"They won't keep his sorry tail in jail more than a few months this time, either," she said, shaking her head. "He'll come out and kill again. They all come out and kill again." Brazell had gone to prison the first time for killing my friend Josephine's mother when Josephine was only two years old.

"Folks downtown don't care about us killing each other," my grandmother said. "They want us to kill each other. They don't need but a few of us to clean up behind them."

Surrounded by boxes of used Christmas ribbon, dingy lace hand-kerchiefs, beltless buckles, and old family photographs, my grand-mother fingered through even more junk—broken jewelry, spent batteries, empty lipsticks, pencil nubs, ink pen caps, screws, foreign coins, wine corks, buttons, bent nails, a beat-up Brownie camera, and a pistol with a scratched barrel.

"They don't even have a picture of Lucy," she said. "That's a shame. Not even a picture of that pretty girl."

I could shoot Brazell, I thought, looking at the gun and not really hearing what my grandmother was saying. But I'd have to find some bullets. Damn! Where would I find bullets?

In the 1950s, when I was growing up on Candy Hill, a camera and a gun were about as useless as junk. No one there had extra money above food and roof to buy film or bullets. Although I was very inter-ested, I pretended not to see the gun.

"History," my grandmother whispered, sorting through odd shapes and sizes of cracked paper with fading images.

Maybe Tony had some bullets at the store, I thought.

"This is the only way you're going to know any of your history," said my grandmother. "'Cause it's yet to turn up in any schoolbook."

I knew Tony had a gun that he kept under the counter.

"If anything about these people ever turns up in any book," my grandmother said, "it won't be until long after I'm dead and gone."

I'd have to trick Tony out of his bullets or steal some. Thinking of the gun, I nestled into a corner at my grandmother's feet and studied each picture as she handed it to me.

"Look at them," she said, handing me another picture. "Your his-tory is dying without saying a word."

What was she talking about now, I wondered, looking at sad faces of great-grandparents, uncles, aunts, cousins, and old friends, dating back to the late 1800s, staring at me.

"Making a picture was serious business," my grandmother said, pointing out one unsmiling dead relative after another and explain-ing their relationships.

What would Tony do if he caught me stealing his bullets? I wondered. And I couldn't walk up to him and ask to borrow a few.

"The closest I got to having my portrait made was a snapshot in a carnival tent," my grandmother said. "Sitting in front of painted scenery with your mother on the arm of a straw chair."

Maybe I could ask Tony to let me use the telephone, so I could get behind the counter, I thought. No, the phone was in the apartment behind the store.

"That's my baby sister and my father standing there behind my mother," my grandmother said, looking down at me. "My mother was a twin. No twins have showed up in this family since."

I hope she doesn't think I'll bring the family twins, I thought, looking at the picture and remembering how big my cousin Earlene had gotten with one baby. The size of her belly didn't worry me nearly as much as the actual delivery. I always had known where babies came from. No stork flew over Candy Hill.

"Some of my prairie people wouldn't take a picture," my grandmother said. "They thought the soul ended up on the paper."

I wanted Brazell's soul smeared somewhere but not on paper, I thought, looking at the gun.

"Most times they had to take pictures in a hurry," my grandmother said, noticing my eyes on the gun. I looked away quickly, but the image of the barrel next to Brazell's head was burned in my mind. I blinked back a tear.

"My papa said there was some kind of law against them owning pictures of themselves back then. I don't know if it was a real law or some lie made up to scare them."

Reading my thoughts, she said, "Seems to me that if you can't get your hands on a bullet, having a gun is harmless."

"Yes, ma'am," I said, hoping she'd hand the pistol to me. Instead, she handed me the camera. "Go shoot somebody with this. I'm not buying you any bullets."

5

◆

Good Old
Golden Rule Days

A Mission for Doll

Television was a round, ten-inch, black-and-white screen full of fog at Mr. Boney's house, and no picture showed on Iola's Main Street in the 1950s. A one-pump filling station and two general stores occupied the town's only intersection. Both stores had hitching posts out front, and each sold varying qualities of cloth by the bolt, nails by the pound, flour and meal by the sacks, eggs by the crate, potatoes by the bushel, beef and pork by the sides, and nails and beans by the scoop.

Iola had no fast food, no slow food, no food to go, no food to stay, and no exotic food. The nearest greasy fried fish was seventy miles away in Houston, and the nearest hamburgers and french fries were thirty miles away at the Bryan Dairy Queen. To some older Iola folks, those limp, lard-drenched fried potatoes might as well have been in France, although I'm certain the French would refuse credit for that recipe. And Iola folk didn't eat their potatoes cooked that way, either. They weren't interested in how other people ate potatoes. Most had never been to a city, and many had no desire ever to go. Although they did spend an occasional out-of-town Saturday night slow dragging to scratched jukebox records in a Railroad Street beer joint at the lower end of downtown Navasota, where migrant workers spent money they earned for toiling all week in Brazos bottom cotton fields.

Livestock had dirty watering holes with green slime. Bees buzzed about their private hives on Mr. Hopkins's farm. But Iola youngsters had no swimming holes or swimming pools, no amusement parks or regular parks, no mini-golf or maxi-golf, no Little League or big league, and no camp—summer or otherwise.

In the 1950s and 1960s, Iola, Texas, was one of my summertime and holiday retreats. To get me away from Candy Hill, my mother often packed me off to Iola for short visits with Aunt Celia's large family. Because no one I knew in Iola had air conditioning, summer heat forced us and everyone else out of the house to catch a breeze and entertain on Saturday nights. Odorless smoke from a barrel of burning cow chips chased mosquitoes and spiraled into a starry sky. Watching smoke disappear above, I saw more stars from Aunt Celia and Uncle Finner Mitchell's aging front porch than I had ever seen anywhere. Sitting for hours gazing up, I hardly noticed weakened boards moving under my bottom when somebody bounced across the floor.

Some evenings we kids caught fireflies and stashed them in a Mason jar. Pairs of curious eyes circled the glass, watching mysterious glows until taillights dimmed. Then we lost interest and bet on which mossy old man playing checkers could spit tobacco farthest from the porch. By sunset, neighbors wandered over, carrying cold drinks and old quilts.

Showtime! Here comes Cousin Roy, everybody howled and pointed down the dusty road at a tiny silhouette struggling to keep his guitar from dragging in the dirt. Rhythmic feet disturbed loose dirt on the grassless lawn, sweaty bodies swayed, and sticky palms clapped when Cousin Roy, eyes closed, sang low-down tune after low-down tune to the out-of-tune blues he picked on a guitar with too few strings.

Iola was a good summertime place for me, my grandmother said, because my mother traveled a lot, carrying my brother to doctors in Houston and Galveston, thumbing rides with friends, relatives, and strangers, too. No doctor discovered why, during his seven-year life, my brother had become so ill after a nurse administered a shot in a routine checkup when he was three months old. "He's so weak he can't hold up his head anymore," I overheard my mother tell my grandmother. "I don't know what they gave him in that needle, but I don't believe my baby will ever walk or talk."

To get to Iola, Uncle George drove on Highway 21 East toward Madisonville, as far as the tiny settlement of North Zulch, where we took Farm Road 39 about ten miles south to Iola. Dotted with farms and fields of cotton and corn, areas around Iola were home to many of our relatives, making it easy for us to catch rides going one way one day and the other way another day.

If a family lived in or near Iola, that family either owned a farm, worked on a farm, or left town. Some families who were not land-owners became migrant workers, hiring themselves out as field hands to plant, chop, pull, and pick cotton. I remember hearing about women field hands in the old days using water breaks to nurse their babies and others becoming mothers between the rows of cotton. Uncle Finner owned a few acres on which he grew a commercial crop of peanuts, harvested by him and his children.

On Saturday mornings, Aunt Celia packed lunch meat and light bread in a cardboard box. The family piled into their old car, little ones sitting on the big ones' laps. Uncle Finner drove them into Bryan to shop. Aunt Celia estimated her children's clothes sizes. They couldn't try clothes on for fit, touch any merchandise, return items for exchange or refund, use public restrooms, or eat in cafes. After the family had shopped, they stopped at our three-room house to visit, eat their sandwiches, and use our two-hole facility in the back-yard, before returning to Iola in the early afternoon.

On Sunday mornings, the Mitchells and their neighbors went to St. Louis Baptist Church, at the same location as Iola's two-room school for colored. Sunday School, singing, preaching, shouting, and tossing coveted coins into collection were followed by box lunch un-der church-yard trees. Children played while men carried boxes to makeshift tables and women arranged food and fanned flies from the fried chicken. We kids were worn out and fell into silent slumber on rear pews long before Rev. Hayward took to the pulpit and preached his evening sermon.

By 1953, the only black children in Iola were my cousins, the Mitchells—Earlene, Charles, Berta Marie, Freddie Mae, Otis Leon, Brenda Kaye, Finner Jr., and J. W.—and two other cousins, Woodrow (Uncle Finner's nephew) and Clifton. Only Earlene, Charles, Berta Marie, Freddie Mae, and Woodrow were of school age. Because Iola required that the school maintain an enrollment of at least five, loss of one student would close Iola's colored school.

One Saturday in June, 1954, before my fifth birthday, Aunt Celia left thirteen-year-old Berta Marie at our house. She didn't feel like shopping that day. When Berta Marie lay across our grandmother's bed in the living room, it became clear to me why everyone called her Doll. Hardly blinking her long black lashes, Doll's huge eyes stared at the wilted flowers on the cracked wallpaper beside the bed until her family returned.

By Monday, Doll was very ill. The closest doctor who would treat her was in Navasota. Uncle Finner begged a day off from his job at the filling station. The doctor said he found nothing. Back home, Doll worsened. Over a two-week period, Aunt Celia and Uncle Finner took Doll back to the doctor several times. Finally, the doctor admitted Doll into the hospital. Before her examination, Doll asked her father to take her home. She said her belly ache had gone away.

After the doctor examined Doll, he told Aunt Celia and Uncle Finner that Doll's problem was her appendix. Uncle Finner held Aunt Celia off the doctor, who said that, although he believed it was too late to save Doll's life, he would perform the surgery, anyway. Hoping for a miracle, the weary couple agreed. To everyone's astonishment, Doll came out of the surgery alive. Later, in a recovery room, though, she whispered to her mother that all she wanted was sleep. Aunt Celia watched Doll fall asleep for the final time.

For weeks, Aunt Celia wept, sometimes in her sleep. Her intense pain was caused by more than grief. Believing that the doctor had neglected Doll, the whole family was bitter.

By the middle of August, the Mitchell children had to face their new plight. Doll's death had released Iola from its obligation to educate its black students. Officials advised the teacher, and they closed the school forever. Aunt Celia and Uncle Finner visited nearby towns. The poorly financed Richards School for Colored accepted their children. Its roof and walls leaked. Light and ventilation were inadequate. Teacher quality was questionable. Out-of-date textbooks were the discarded property of other schools. And there was no public transportation.

Uncle Finner bought an old car hull, rebuilt an engine, and taught Charles and Earlene to drive. Uneasy about her children's safety since she lost Doll, Aunt Celia worried. Wringing her hands, she peeked through the porch screen periodically and watched Uncle Finner work on that old car until the children's dreaded first day of school in Richards. Accepting her children's new routine with great apprehension, Aunt Celia cried after they left and fretted until they returned.

On chilly mornings, Earlene helped Aunt Celia make oatmeal and biscuits. Freddie Mae helped pack sack lunches. Charles was by his father's side, checking tires and oil. Woodrow met them out front, and they were on the highway before first light. For most of the school year, night still rested on the Iola white school when the Mitchell children passed on their way to the Richards School for Colored. Traveling sixty miles a day, round-trip, in rain, fog, or ice and almost always in darkness, my cousins drove home past the Iola white school, where night already had fallen. With their right to an education threatened by their sister's death, my cousins made going to school a mission for Doll.

After Earlene's 1957 graduation and Charles' 1958 graduation, Woodrow took over the driving. By then, the rest of the Mitchell children and Clifton were in school, too. When I had vacation days, I went to school with them. My school was the lowest quality Bryan offered, but it was better than the school my cousins drove sixty miles a day to attend. Because of something to do with taxes, in 1961 my cousins had to change from Richards to Normangee, a change that did not provide an improvement in schools.

When Woodrow moved away in 1962, Freddie Mae became the driver, until she graduated in May, 1964. In June, 1964, Iola officials visited Aunt Celia and Uncle Finner. In light of civil rights developments, they invited Otis Leon, Brenda Kaye, Finner Jr., J. W., and Clifton to attend school in Iola. After ten years of out-of-town schools, Uncle Finner and Aunt Celia accepted, but not without reservations. Aunt Celia's fears that her children would be mistreated were alleviated somewhat when Iola teachers and students seemed to be making a sincere effort to welcome them. Brenda Kaye, Finner Jr., J. W., and Clifton graduated from Iola High School. Otis Leon attended the school for one year before his death in 1965 in the Madisonville Hospital, after complications arising from surgery on a broken leg he suffered at football practice. Next to the closed colored school, Otis Leon—like Doll before him—was eulogized at St. Louis Baptist Church, where Earlene had been married in 1959. Until 1976, family reunions enlivened the church property annually. Friends and relatives said so long to Uncle Finner there in 1982. By the time Aunt Celia died in 1987, however, Iola city government had assumed management of the school and church property and had established it as the city's garbage dump.

Though the Mitchells boast no war heroes or superstars, presidents or inventors, diplomats or millionaires, among them there are no dropouts, quitters, or losers—an extraordinary feat at a time when the world didn't care. For that small achievement, the world will build them no monument. But beneath Iola's discarded plastic cups, broken glass, half-eaten lunches, and old newspapers, the earth embraces a family's dreams and the memories of a thousand quiet smiles.

Grace for the Graceful

There we were, skinny eight-year-olds, strutting around on our red gravel playground behind muscular, six-foot-three Mr. Pruitt.

Every day after school, we spread out the tumbling mats for practice. None of us minded staying an hour or so before going home. There was nothing else of interest to do on Candy Hill. I could go home with Dora Jackson and watch her fry chicken for her sisters and brothers, if it was her night to cook. I could go to Joan Robertson's house, sip iced tea, and look at old photographs that her mother kept handy for visitors. Or I could go to the Hines's house before Mrs. Hines got home from work and watch Mr. Hines feed his chickens.

"Before you little ladies learn any gymnastics routines or positions, you have to learn poise, posture, walking, sitting, and standing," Mr. Pruitt explained, motioning us to fall in behind him. "Let's keep walking."

In the 1950s, the world had hardly heard the word *gymnastics*. But Mr. Pruitt ordered this little book from someplace in Europe, I think, with stick figures in it showing positions for certain tumbling and floor routines. We had seen him studying that little book over his lunch and had heard through the school grapevine that he would be picking a very small, select group to train for his team.

"Hold your chins up, ladies," he called over his shoulder.

The classes at Washington Elementary School—first through seventh grades—took turns on the playground. The area wasn't large enough for every class to do everything they wanted at the same time. Some days, Mr. Pruitt took portable bases out of storage for a class to play softball. Other days, we played basketball on our dirt court or kicked up a cloud practicing our drill-team steps. On rainy days, we stood quietly around classroom windows watching puddles form under the swings in the middle of the schoolyard.

This particular day, Mr. Pruitt had taken tumbling mats from storage and placed them on the grass under a thick canopy of trees at the end of the playground nearest the cafeteria. Oh, that little cafeteria building always smelled so good. We had real food for lunch—peaches that still had their fuzz, mashed potatoes that started out with their own skins, gravy that did not come from a jar, meat that was all meat and not part soy. The school nurse tested vision and hearing in the cafeteria. We hated it when nurse came in the morning. Hungry for lunch, we called out tiny letters and listened to high whistles while we smelled candied yams, steak smothered in onion gravy, collard greens, and cornbread baking in the oven.

Excited by having something new to do, many girls were afraid that Mr. Pruitt's tumbling and gymnastics team would be picked based on who had the longest ponytail or the lightest skin or whose parents were schoolteachers. Well, those things might have counted with some teachers, but not with Mr. Pruitt. "You have to put that hair up," he said to me one day. "I don't want you getting tangled up in it and strangling yourself."

Mr. Pruitt wasn't impressed by anything but good straight headstands and walkovers. Having been a track star in college, he knew all about muscles and joints and didn't require all of us to do the same things. As a matter of fact, he said, the fastest way to be thrown out of the activity was to try something he'd warned was dangerous for your body type.

It didn't take him long to pick out the girls who could do the routines in his little book of stick figures. We astounded the audience at our first performance. The Kemp Gymnasium was packed when we rolled out our mats and took the floor. Mr. Pruitt stood far enough to the side where he thought we couldn't see him. But I saw a wide grin creep across his face when I came out of my handstand.

A Relic of Segregation

I heard the sweet unseasoned sounds of saxophones and snares bouncing off the side of Kemp's gymnasium. Walking up West Nineteenth Street, now West Martin Luther King, I turned the corner by Littleton's Snack Bar and headed toward West Twentieth Street, to the Kemp High School campus.

I was just entering sixth grade at Washington Elementary School in the fall of 1960. All I could do at that time was dream of one day marching with the band, twirling a baton, or cheering from the sidelines wearing a short maroon skirt and a white sweater with a capital K on the front.

A drop of rain fell on my face. Hoping that it would really rain, I climbed onto wooden slat seats at the football field. It was too hot to follow the band into the tin barn of a gymnasium at the far end of the field, if they had to continue rehearsal inside. I was excited watching fewer than twenty members move in a simple formation on the field, led by an impressive line of tassel-booted, baton-tossing, hip-swinging majorettes with smiles gleaming from innocent smooth brown faces.

Most of the poor families who lived around the school had no money for band instruments or uniforms. In fact, many Kemp students hired themselves out in summer to local plantations as cotton-field workers to earn money for school clothes and to help the family meet routine expenses. Participation in the school band and other activities required that the school provide instruments, equipment, and those uniforms that could not be homemade.

Dependent on Stephen F. Austin High School for hand-me-down horns, Kemp band members ended up with mostly reed instruments and very little brass. Using raw talent and worn-out horns with chipped finishes that had lost their tone and their ability to shine, Mr. Webster, the band director, created an ensemble of uniquely mature and entertaining musicians who laid down the hottest jazz and blues licks in the district. Although the football team was a consistent loser, every other Friday night, the air around the Kemp football field was filled with hot dog smells and the sound of the band rocking the bleachers with spontaneous jamming.

My cousin Lee White, who lived along the Graveyard Line, had started at Kemp High the year I was born, 1949. He was only thirteen when he began walking several miles to attend eighth-grade classes at Kemp. Lee said his excitement wilted after he was selected for the football team and spent several days watching Coach Scurry pick through and try to salvage sports equipment discarded by Stephen F. Austin.

"I expected to have old desks and old books," he said. "I don't know why I was surprised to see old worn-out football pads. I guess because I was five-foot-seven and weighed only 119 pounds! I needed lots of good padding!"

Traveling to out-of-town games on a bus with missing seats that was known to break down, the Kemp band didn't have enough instruments to go around. Ridiculed by students in other towns, Kemp High band members spread far apart, proudly filling out their formation lines while some marched empty-handed during the half-time activities.

Lee said he decided not to play basketball. Having no gymnasium meant he would be playing on dirt like he had for seven years at Washington Elementary School. "Around 1950," Lee said, "a large metal building was erected. The students were glad to get a gym so we could come in out of the rain."

During the 1950s and 1960s, the tin barn served as shelter for basketball games, physical education programs, festivals, band rehearsals, pep rallies, and other activities that attracted large crowds. Ventilated by crank-out windows high on the walls and an industrial fan at one end, the facility was referred to by some students as "the barbecue pit."

Recycled Schoolbooks

I stomped through the front door angrily and slammed my school-books on the floor. "Why can't we ever get clean books with all the pages?" I shouted. "They got these books out of the trash!"

School had started less than a week ago, and my teachers were still scrambling to find enough books with enough pages to issue to their students. Several softly frayed pages of my worn sixth-grade geography book were torn, and a couple of pages were missing altogether. Almost every page of another book had been defaced with the smooth black lead of a sharp pencil, and obscene words and racial slurs were scribbled in its margins.

I sat down on the floor in the middle of the mess I'd made and dropped my face into my hands. "Why even bother going to school! I'll never get to be anything I want to be anyway!"

"That's how some people want you to feel." My grandmother looked at me sadly. "Give up, be a dummy, and prove them right."

"What does it matter if I know how to conjugate a verb?" I asked. "Or divide by fractions and use decimal points?"

"They're out there," my grandmother said, "praying you'll fail, so when things in this country do change, you still won't get to be what you want to be because you won't know how."

Could she be right? I wondered, as she left the room.

"Take this," my grandmother said, returning. She handed me a pencil with an eraser. "Rub out what you can. Ignore the rest."

I picked up the books and went out on the porch. Fall had turned cool that September of 1961. Shadows grew longer and longer, as the sun disappeared behind the pointed tin roof of Miss Gladys's tiny house across the street. Miss Gladys, not long before, had come home from work, where she spent the day cleaning and cooking for a family across town. Her little black dog sniffed and wagged when she brought out his bowl.

"Do good in school this year," she called to me.

I was erasing the margins of the book when Miss Geneva passed on her way home from working in somebody's kitchen. Tucked under her arm were her purse and a brown paper sack that probably held the scraps of the dinner she'd just served.

"Try to make all A's this year," Miss Geneva called to me.

I never resisted or even questioned becoming an educated person. I knew, however, by looking around at my Candy Hill neighbors that education alone would not allow me to make a decent living, with options in Bryan so few. Lots of Candy Hill high school graduates wouldn't be considered for a position as a five-and-dime clerk or a waitress in a greasy spoon.

As the cool breeze swept evening into the night, I finished erasing the pages and took the books back into the house. My grandmother cleared a space on the kitchen table and told me to do my homework.

The Reference Books

My mother rushed in through the front door that evening as if she had a mission. Usually, after getting home from work, she'd pour a cup of coffee and sit down at the kitchen table. My grandmother and I would join her to talk about what had happened during the day. About sundown, my father would come home from working on his farm, and we all would have dinner together.

"In sixth grade," she began as she walked in and put her things down on the chair by the door, "lessons get harder. And they don't get any easier throughout high school."

School hasn't even started yet, I thought; why is she spoiling my last few days of summer? She went over to a small bookcase in the corner, knelt in front of it, and started taking off the whatnots. One by one, she removed the little ceramic pieces from their nesting places.

"You're going to have to write papers about places we've never been. And do research on subjects we don't know about."

Not believing my ears, I couldn't believe my mother had just admitted to me that there were things in the world that she didn't know. I had sense enough to know that no one knew everything. But my mother never had had a problem helping me with my homework. My friends would gather at our house to do their assignments, too, so my mother could help them. She knew the answers to all the questions we'd ever asked about people and places, because she was always reading about an exotic location. Unlike many of my Candy Hill friends' parents, some of whom were virtually illiterate, my mother was smarter than many of my elementary school teachers.

"Get me a small box to put these things in," she said. "Be sure it has tissue paper to wrap these things up."

With no idea what she was doing or why, I went to her private stash of boxes in different sizes and shapes that she kept in a corner of her bedroom. My mother collected sturdy, stackable boxes. A house with no closets may have presented other people with an impossible storage problem. To my mother, however, a shortage of storage space was a healthy challenge to her organizational skills. I selected a box, checked to see if there was tissue paper inside, and took it to her.

"Here," she said. "Wrap these and place them in the box."

"Why are you moving these things?" I wrapped the first piece carefully and placed it in the box.

"The encyclopedia man is coming tonight," she said. "If we buy his books, we'll need these shelves."

"We have encyclopedias in the school library," I said.

"I know that," said my mother. "But they're out of date and have pages missing. Besides, those books have to stay at school. I need books here. But you can use them, too."

The First Thanksgiving

I walked into the school cafeteria with the rest of my sixth-grade class-mates. Steam clouded my eyeglasses, but the delicious aromas failed to arouse my passion for a feast.

Because no finer Thanksgiving meal could be consumed anywhere in town in 1961, school officials from the central office consistently chose to visit our campus for Thanksgiving lunch. Several dark-suited men sat at tiny tables in the Washington Elementary School cafeteria, greedily shoveling down turkey, dressing, gravy, green beans, cran-berry sauce, hot buttered rolls, and sweet-potato pie, as if this would be their last supper.

At our school, lunch on any other day was prepared with the same care as the traditional Thanksgiving lunch. Counter surfaces sparkled. Utensils gleamed. Floors were polished to a high gloss. Wearing snowy uniforms and nets over their hair, the women who prepared our meals looked as sterile as nurses, handled food with a certain reverence, and delivered healthy portions to everyone in line. After all of the students and faculty had eaten, the cooks packed what they hadn't served into neat parcels and distributed the boxes to children they knew would have no dinner otherwise.

The lunch line was long that day because all of the students were served a traditional Thanksgiving menu, whether they had twenty-five cents to pay for the food or not. I seemed to be the only person in the cafeteria picking over the tasty meal, leaving most of it swimming in cold gravy. After lunch, I bid my friends farewell and left my crayon-colored, mimeographed, fan-tailed turkey gobbling on the bulletin board until Monday. All the way home from school that afternoon, I thought about my teacher's account of the first Thanksgiving, which she insisted had been created by Native Americans and not the Pil-grims, who came to America after Columbus stumbled onto these shores by mistake.

"The first Thanksgiving would have been the last for the strangers who had come from across the sea, if not for the generosity of tribal people who found the camp of destitute travelers and brought them food," Mrs. King had said, walking up and down the aisles. "Later, the Indians taught the strangers to trap wild game and to grow and harvest corn. They tried to make friends with the travelers." We all stared at our teacher in disbelief. How could she say that about Thanksgiving?

"There are tribal accounts that these strangers from across the sea were so close to starvation on that first so-called Thanksgiving, they were considering eating their own dead." We all stopped breathing, and finally the lunch bell interrupted the long, uncomfortable silence.

"Class is dismissed," said Mrs. King. "Have a happy Thanksgiving." We were too stunned to move. "Class is dismissed," she said again. "I'll see you all on Monday. Don't eat too much in the cafeteria."

Throughout lunch, I didn't want talk to anyone. My classmate, Henry Hammond Hill, asked for my sweet-potato pie. Wondering why we always called him by his full name, I gave him the pie and spent the rest of the lunch hour sitting at the noisy table picking over my turkey and dressing and cranberry sauce and thinking about Mrs. King's account of Thanksgiving.

Could it be true? I was so confused. The encyclopedias that my mother had bought didn't say the Indians had been responsible for the first Thanksgiving. Surely if Indians had invented Thanksgiving or anything else, my grandmother would have told me. After all, those were her people. No, not the ones the Pilgrims met. Different ones. Suddenly unsure of everything I thought I knew about myself and my world, I panicked. My head was full of questions with no answers.

My grandmother was in the kitchen when I walked into the house. "Who's responsible for Thanksgiving?" I demanded.

"Whoever has the food," she said, staring at me curiously.

The Letter

The afternoon darkened early that day. Distant thunder from a storm brewing somewhere south of Bryan rushed me home from school—no dropping by Billie Jean's house to ogle her handsome older brother, Joe Nathan; no stopping at the Jacksons's to play; no tea cakes at Peaches and Wanda's; and definitely no detours through the cemetery.

I wasn't afraid of storms. Actually, I loved them. But I wanted to be at home where I could feel cozy and safe with rain beating on the roof and wind pushing against the walls. A couple of raindrops hit my face, and I sped up, thinking how badly my day had gone at school. Arguing with my sixth-grade substitute teacher about a math problem had been a mistake, even if her answer was wrong! No, especially if her answer was wrong! She sent me and my right answer to the office, where our principal, Mr. Sadberry, was glad to see me. Sitting at the receptionist's desk, he smiled and shoved the student roll reports he'd been working on at me.

"Finish these, answer the telephone, and do your homework." He went into his inner office and closed the door.

In 1961, Washington Elementary School didn't have a secretary, full-time or otherwise. During their free periods, teachers shared office duties with the principal and smart-mouthed students like me. The telephone didn't ring often, but if it did, my frequent office experiences had taught me to answer politely, handle the calls, and operate the public address and paging systems.

When I walked into our house, my grandmother reached into her apron pocket and handed me an envelope. My fingers trembled when I took the letter, thick with several pages and possibly a photograph. Besides letters from cousins and friends, I got letters and pictures from penpals in New York, Philadelphia, California, Chicago, Mississippi, and Florida, plus occasional postcards from Europe and the South Pacific. The network had started with my Mississippi friend, whose father, stationed for a time at Bryan Air Force Base, had been reassigned. She wrote me with the addresses of her new friends who also traveled with their fathers to military installations all over the world.

My mother didn't mind that I spent my errand money on stamps. She said that receiving letters, photographs, and picture postcards was the next best thing to traveling to exotic places, walking on sandy beaches, sliding down snowy slopes, strolling among skyscrapers, and dreaming of things that Candy Hill could not offer me. I couldn't believe my eyes as I scanned the name of my newest penpal, his Boston address, the round red postmark, and a canceled four-cent stamp.

"I hope that letter's from a boy and not a soldier!" my grandmother warned. "I don't want some grown man showing up looking for you."

Fighting for the Lead

I was alone on the street except for a skinny dog trotting along with his nose to the wet ground, looking for a scrap to eat. An occasional driver rushing home from work splashed me when the car tires hit muddy puddles in the road. There'd been talk of paving streets on Candy Hill. But as late as the 1960s, talk of paving Candy Hill streets was still just talk.

Rain the day before had left a lingering gray sky and the air heavy with moisture. My light sweater had proven insufficient protection against the cool, damp autumn air. My arms surrendered to cramps from carrying heavy schoolbooks, which every student had to take home every day, because our school had no lockers or space for lockers. Lockers would not have mattered. My mother would have insisted I bring the books home anyway.

I was late coming home after rehearsing for the Christmas recital with Mrs. King, my music and home room teacher. It was only November, but she had assured the entire school and other schools in and around town that this program would be a real production. My rehearsal could not have been worse. Poor concentration. I hadn't been able to hit the high notes or remember all the verses of "Silent Night."

"Your voice is weak today," Mrs. King said during rehearsal. "Are you doing the voice exercises I gave you?"

"Yes, ma'am," I lied. I hadn't sung one scale that day, the day before, or any other day.

"Please share with me what's wrong?" she asked in her most formal tone. "If you don't improve, I'll have to replace you."

Could I tell Mrs. King that a boy in my class had brought whiskey to school in a Coke bottle? Could I tell her that the girl who would have gotten the vocal lead, if not for me, drank the liquor? Could I tell Mrs. King that the girl promptly had scheduled a fight with me if I didn't sing badly, so she could get the vocal lead? I wasn't afraid to fight. I'd fought before. Everyone I knew had been in fights. My drunken neighbors fought every Saturday night, and some even killed each other.

Although I wasn't willing to die for a singing part, I wasn't going to deliberately lose it because I was afraid to fistfight the competition. Walking toward home, I sang the scales Mrs. King had given me. I'd made my decision.

Two, Four, Six, Eight!

It was just dusk when I ran into the house without dusting the residue from our unpaved road off my shoes on the mat outside the door. I was so angry.

"Wipe your feet," said my grandmother.

"Two, four, six, eight," I said, stepping out of the door and stomping on the mat. "They don't want to integrate, is what they were yelling! And they threw eggs! Don't they know I don't want to be with them, either?"

Images surrounded me and reminded me that having dreams was a risky thing. Headlines sprawled across newspapers shouted that I'd be killed if I tried to vote. Of course, being only eleven years old at the time, I knew I couldn't vote. But my grandmother could vote, couldn't she? And what about my mother and father? They voted, didn't they? I didn't know if they did.

Jumpy black-and-white pictures on the television assured me that I'd be arrested if I tried to eat in a restaurant downtown. I didn't care about eating at a restaurant. I just wanted to be able to use the restroom when my mother and I were out shopping. Because I loved my teachers at Washington Elementary, I wasn't interested in going to any other schools. I just wanted to be issued a textbook that had all the pages.

In the house, I rushed into the bedroom. What was I looking for, I wondered—that old golf club my grandmother kept by her bed when I was a little girl. Protection, she used to say. I fell to my knees looking under the bed, remembering that I hadn't seen the club since I was six. What about that pistol she kept in a shoebox? Last winter, I saw her put it into a dresser drawer. I'll be ready the next time they cruise into Candy Hill yelling at me and throwing eggs, I thought, opening a drawer.

"What are you doing?" my grandmother asked, surprising me.

"I want to hurt them!" I said.

"You should want to hurt them," she said sarcastically. "You've been through so much suffering over all the years of your long, dreadful life of hard work and bad treatment. You deserve to go out and hurt somebody. And have somebody hurt you back. Your mother will be so proud of you."

"What am I supposed to do?" I begged, aching deep inside.

My grandmother said seriously, "You must learn control."

"What about them learning control?" I asked, relieved that she was not making fun of me. "They need to learn how to act."

"What other people learn or don't learn isn't my concern," my grandmother said, leaving the room.

My eyes rested on her lacy white slips, folded neatly in the dresser drawer. In each corner of the compartment, she'd arranged sweet-smelling pouches of body powder and scented soaps. Peeking out from under a stack of embroidered handkerchiefs, the handle of her pistol momentarily caught my attention. Without disturbing it, I closed the drawer quietly.

6

◆

Merry Christmas, Baby

Christmas Is for the Children

Our Candy Hill neighborhood buzzed with holiday cheer in 1954. The houses on our block, playing the same radio station, filled the air with angelic voices and assaulted my four-year-old ears with advertisements of treats we couldn't afford. That was before we moved into the corner cottage, before my mother married, and before her consistent work history established good lines of credit in downtown Bryan department stores.

Everyone in the neighborhood seemed to be struck by the spirit. Mrs. Raper, who never spoke to children, traipsed around like an overweight good fairy, passing out sugary wishes tucked inside red woolen Santa booties. Mrs. Hines, who wouldn't allow a thirsty child a warm drink of water from her yard faucet in the heat of summer, tried to distribute homemade cookies to suspicious Candy Hill youngsters, who were unable to eat the goodies for fear that they might be laced with poison.

Operators of grocery stores in other parts of town gave needy Candy Hill families last-minute, nearly-gone-bad holiday turkeys after regular customers had finished their shopping. And more fortunate well-wishers brought carloads of broken toy fire trucks with chipping red paint, bicycles that needed chains, sweaters with small holes in the elbows, toy tea sets with missing saucers, and naked, one-eyed dolls.

My mother, who detested hand-me-downs and other people's discarded junk, politely told the good-willers to keep going. Although some of their offerings looked somewhat interesting to me, I didn't mind that she passed on the stuff. I wasn't very fond of toys. Thoughtfully, she decorated our tiny Christmas tree, whose most important branches were absent. Filling in the middle of the tree with ribbons of recycled green crepe paper, she carefully planned the spaces in between, hanging frosty white plastic icicles all over the tree and paying close attention to the area near the base. Meticulously, her graceful fingers started at the top of the tree, sprinkling make-believe snowflakes over every branch. Then her smooth, slender hands added a few shiny red balls. Finally, she was ready to finish the job. She opened a small box and offered me something wrapped in white tissue.

"Want to put the star on the tree so Santa Claus will come to see you tonight?" she asked me. "You know Santa won't come unless there is a star on the tree."

Putting on that star meant I'd have to get up and walk over to the tree. The house had been cold all that day, and the wood supply looked low. Wind whipped at our thin walls and found narrow openings around unsealed windows and loose-fitting doors. The only place I was inclined to go was the kitchen, where I could nestle up to a hot stove and steal tastes of my grandmother's cake batter. I shivered. Declining, I shook my head and stayed warmly tucked in a chair with a quilt around my feet and legs.

My mother unwrapped a white star laden with silver glitter and fragments of pearl. A little impatiently, she stuck the star on the top of the tree. "You know I'm only doing this for you and your brother. Christmas is for children."

Busy stringing colored lights across the front window behind the tree, she sang "Jingle Bells" along with the radio, asking herself out loud from time to time why I wouldn't help her carry the tune.

Christmas Eve

I lay awake, tucked warmly into bed on that Christmas Eve of 1958, listening to the breaking limbs of trees burdened with ice. Those

sounds gave the night a frightening quality, like someone was scream-
ing, and then the limbs went crashing to the ground. I wasn't afraid,
though. Bigmama was asleep in the other room. We had moved from
our wood-heated rent house and into our comfortably warm, gas-
heated corner cottage with indoor plumbing, running water in the
kitchen, and a living room that did not serve double duty as a
bedroom.

My mother had gone to an engagement party with my father. They
were to be married on New Year's Eve. I had wanted to go to the party,
but double mumps confined me to bed. My face looked as if it were
about to explode. I could hardly open my mouth wide enough eat
and brush my teeth. Everyone assured me that I wouldn't recover in
time for the wedding.

Still sad and detached after my brother had died in October of that
year, recovery seemed remote to me. Our sweet little cottage and
everything in it seemed changed, the rooms smaller and darker. To
keep from hurting so much, I tried not to remember my brother, his
pain, my mother's pain. I wondered how she would go on living, having lost one she loved so much. I knew I would never be able to fill
that hole in her life.

Convulsions had taken over my brother's body the day before he
died. My mother held him in her arms that night, while I lay awake
in the next room, feeling guilty that I was the healthy one. When I got
up the next morning, my mother was still holding my brother. While
I was getting ready for school, my mother was still holding his frail
body. When I eased out the front door wearing mismatched clothes,
my mother was still holding him. Unnoticed, I quietly closed the door,
went down the steps, and walked to school in a daze. I had not slept
for two nights.

From my spot in the family car, I watched the back of the hearse
where my brother's body was. Uncertain where the rest of him might
be, I knew the hearse had only his body. Holes in the bumpy road
grabbed at the hearse's rear tires, but the slow, heavy vehicle man-

aged to bounce out each time. My body movements were confined to my thundering heart and my eyes, darting from the corner of my cat-eye glasses. I caught a glimpse of my mother's face, a mixture of beauty, confusion, pain, and relief.

That Christmas season, Candy Hill was frozen as firmly as my own heart. From the window near my bed, I saw white frost blanketing the ground. Tire ruts had hardened in the muddy road. Icicles dangled from roof edges. Mr. Hines's chickens never left their roost. And for the entire Christmas vacation week, none of the neighborhood children played in the streets. Everyone was somewhere trying to keep warm, and that was not easy for some of my neighbors, whose tiny rent houses had paper-thin plank walls with no covering on the outside and not much inside covering walls or floors.

Candy Hill mothers and grandmothers still crafted bed quilts from scraps of the family's old clothing, for occasions as cold as this. In the summer, young neighborhood girls went from house to house with their scissors, to see who needed help cutting quilt squares. There was always a glass of cold lemonade and sweet tea cakes while we sat on the porch chatting after we'd finished. By hand, women sewed the quilt pieces together into elaborate star patterns or flower blocks or other bursts of color.

The mother of one of my playmates tied neatly cut strips left from quilt squares into rugs to cover bare floors and made matching fabric jams to cram under drafty doors. She also wrapped an old sofa and chair in hand-made slipcovers that matched ruffled curtains and throw pillows she made from bed sheets, trimmed with quilt scraps. Tasteful calendar pictures were tacked strategically over holes in the wall. A rusty floor lamp with a dingy shade stood in the corner behind the chair. Books, family snapshots, and soda bottles of plastic flowers, cloaked in crocheted holders and set on wooden boxes, finished the decor.

Every room in their house was papered with newsprint, tacked in corners and taped along seams. When the wind blew, the paper rattled.

A small, pot-bellied, wood-burning heater in a corner of the living room was the only source of warmth, but somehow the house stayed warm. Maybe it was the stove pushing out heat under a pot of great-smelling food that kept the house so warm, or perhaps it was the brothers and sisters laughing at each other's silly jokes and playing checkers on that hand-tied rug made of knotted fragments of their own clothing. They didn't know they were poor and didn't care what—if anything—was under a Christmas tree.

Another frozen tree branch broke outside, reminding me how cold and vicious the weather would be on Christmas Day. But I didn't worry. My friends' world was safe. My own world, though in transition as I still grieved for my brother, was secure in the promise of having as much of my family together in one house as I could, even if I didn't go to my mother and father's wedding. After all, most people never had that opportunity, anyway.

The Day After Christmas

The sky was hazy that Friday, December 26, 1958. Hanging low just above the houses, dense, moist gray clouds spawned a fine cold mist that drifted to the ground, freezing everything it touched. Pointed tin rooftops and tall leafless trees glistened in the distance like Colorado postcards. Nearer the ground, electrical wires sagged under the weight of ice, and the slippery front steps of our house and the porches of our Candy Hill neighbors shimmered under a frosty crust. Still ill with the mumps, I could do nothing but read and look out of the window.

The house smelled of peppermint, oranges, turkey, nutmeg, and, of course, cedar; but our small brown Christmas tree had shed nearly all its tiny dried branches, leaving little to hold up the sparkling red balls my mother had so carefully placed upon them. Fear of burning down our house had prompted her to stop the flashing of colorful lights on Christmas night. My grandmother had warned her that she was putting up the tree too early.

Through our living room window, when my grandmother let me out of bed for a few minutes that day, I noticed nothing moving on the street—not a person, not a car, not a dog or cat. I didn't expect to see a cat out in wretched weather, not the way they tiptoed around lightly in a spring shower, trying to keep their feet from touching the ground and getting wet.

No one I knew personally, except a yellow-slickered trash man who lived around the corner, owned the proper winter clothing to be out that day after Christmas. The winter before, a storm had blown in while I was at school. My woolen overcoat absorbed cold moisture and soaked my sweater underneath. I came down with the flu. The cough hung on until spring.

At times, my clear plastic rain slicker kept out rain but welcomed cold that seemed to chill me to the bone. On East Nineteenth Street, now East Martin Luther King Street, the students' main route to Washington Elementary School on East Twentieth Street, mud was so thick and sticky that it pulled off our shoes and sent us home in soggy socks. During entire winters when I was a child, my toes stayed cold. I was plagued with sore throat and lost my voice every other week.

It was my guess that, by this time, our Candy Hill neighbors—after tossing out their shiny gift paper and picking their turkeys clean—were huddled around a pot-bellied wood stove or a kerosene heater or a gas jet burner, trying to keep warm.

I can't remember what was in the box with my name on it; presents didn't matter to me that year, and Christmas dinner was a blur alone in my bed. I was preoccupied with the loss of my brother. His seventh birthday would have been December 26, had he not died a few months before. Our one-day-late Christmas gift, as my mother always called him fondly, was gone. And my broken heart was not prepared for any festivity or joyous celebration.

My hot breath fogged the window pane. I traced fragile stick figures on the slick surface with my fingertip. Through my delicate drawings, I saw a lonely road out front.

Visitor

My father's '57 Ford turned off the narrow country road, crossed a cattle guard, and made a slow, bumpy approach toward a white picket fence about a quarter of a mile away. A brick chimney pushed white puffs high above the grove of evergreens that nestled neatly near the wraparound porch of the modest house.

There were no neighbors! As far as the eye could see, there was nothing but land, trees, and sky. Cows greeted the car and followed attentively near the rear bumper. Hanging out with my father on the farm over the last year, I'd come closer to a cow than I ever been, seeing its nostrils flare and wondering how it could walk in a straight line with eyes so awkwardly placed. Magazine pictures made cows look like ugly people. Elsie the Cow popped into my head, standing up on high-heeled hooves and wearing a crisp apron.

I'd never been to a real Christmas celebration until 1959. Oh, we always had a big meal and people came by, but this was different. I was skeptical of the celebration, because I knew Santa Claus was a phony. Every kid who lived on Candy Hill knew that. Holidays made us feel lonelier and poorer. Personally, I found it difficult to tie the whole Santa thing and the Jesus thing together. They just didn't fit in the same picture, and no one could adequately explain to me how they should. I couldn't accept both, so I discarded Santa Claus.

Although my fragile ten-year-old feelings still winced at not being included in my parents' wedding nearly a year ago, for the sake of this new family arrangement, I'd play along. I never understood why they didn't simply change the wedding day! They knew I had the mumps. It wasn't like they had a big traditional wedding—no church, no flowers, no rings, no reception, no honeymoon. For awhile, I thought they might have been rushing to marry because my mother was pregnant. She wasn't.

I was convinced that I'd have a terrible time on the beautiful farm that a great-grandfather had begun purchasing in the 1880s, when he was tenderly entering manhood. At his death, because his wife already had died, their children, including my father's father, inherited, divided, and inhabited the property. Gramps periodically—and often painfully, from a financial standpoint—added to his fifty-acre portion until he had acquired more than two hundred acres. Money to make the payment was scraped from every hiding place.

About twenty miles away from Bryan, the farm was situated between Old San Antonio Road and Tabor Road, near the tiny communities of Edge and Wheelock. A valid landmark in Texas history, this route was traveled by Bigmama's prairie people when they roamed and raided throughout Texas all the way to Mexico. Bigmama didn't go with us to the Christmas celebration. She and Aunt Sis had gone to Carlos to spend the holiday with their sister Leatha and their brother-in-law Dan, whom they both despised.

My father pulled in close to the fence to save space for other cars. Gramps' two elderly hunting hounds loped toward the car and escorted us to the porch. Gramps' woebegone dogs hadn't had a meaningful hunt in more than ten years. Folds of skin over Andy's eyes prevented him from seeing more than two or three inches in the distance. Sal had lost most of his teeth and couldn't eat anything if he caught it.

My leather-booted foot found the first step of the porch. As hard as I fought against them, warm feelings filled me. Once I was inside the house, my nostrils stretched to capacity, enjoying those wonderful smells—spiced sweets, fruits, and turkey. Welcoming us, Gramps got up from his rocking chair. He'd been poking the fire and waiting for the descent of his huge family.

I wandered over to the corner by the window that held a magnificent cedar Christmas tree, so out of place in somebody's living room. Of course, in our neighborhood, nobody's living room would hold a tree that big. The decorations were to be put in place by the grandchildren after everyone arrived. My father said Gram supervised this delicate annual operation. My father said Gram refused to buy ornaments. Buzzing around the kitchen, singing to the rhythm of her cooking noises, she insisted that everything on the Christmas tree must be edible—ropes of popcorn, cookie stars, candy balls, nuts, peppermint canes, and other delicious morsels.

Gram smiled when she saw me and gave me a hug. "Where have you been all of my life?" she asked every time I saw her.

We could hear automobile engines outside. The rest of the family was driving up the lane. I ran to the door and looked out the side window. The cars were passing the big old oak tree that held a summertime swing—a heavy rope with a truck tire dangling at the end. Gramps flung open the door as soon as the first foot hit the porch. Excited greetings and tight hugs were followed by sloppy kisses and my-how-you've-growns. Suddenly, there was a mountain of colorfully wrapped presents under the still undecorated tree. The house, bulging at its seams to accommodate the crowd, roared with laughter. Gramps poured warm drinks. I was an outsider. No one knew me. There were so many people in the house, no one noticed me. I went to the kitchen and helped Gram bring the edible tree ornaments into the dining room. The grownups gathered around the fire and talked, while the kids ate Gram's decorations. I knew they shouldn't be eating them, but I didn't know if I was allowed to say anything. Gram and I did manage to hang a few on the tree.

The weather turned colder that night. The wind stirred the trees. I followed Gramps to the firebox on the porch for more firewood.

My ears strained to hear the light murmur of falling ice. What an odd sound, I thought, like the whisper of distant angels. I guessed that the sound was unique to the country; I'd never heard it in my neighborhood.

"Gramps, look," I said, pointing to the road beyond the lane. "Do you see it?"

He stared. A dim yellow light moved slowly in the distance through the haze of the night. "Yes, I see it," he said softly.

"What is it?" I asked.

"Just someone passing," he answered calmly.

The dry wood crackled as we dropped fresh logs on the glowing embers. The family surprised me when they beckoned for me to join them in singing carols. Aunt Leslie's voice cracked in "Silent Night." Gram had prepared beds in a back room for the children. We got into our designated beds, and she turned out the light.

"I want all of you to go to sleep, or Santa Claus won't come to visit any of you," Gram said, leaving the room.

I got up, walked to the window, and looked at the small patch of ground outside that my father said would be a cornfield next spring. I felt lost and confused among all these strangers. I pressed my face so close to the cold windowpane that my warm breath left a fog on the glass, blurring my vision. Then I saw movement outside. I wiped a clear spot on the pane and strained to see. A dark figure with a load on its back moved up the lane by the yellow glow of a lantern. "Somebody's out there," I said.

The other children flung themselves from their beds, ran to the window, and stood behind me, watching the figure move closer to the picket fence. It stopped, set down the lantern, and changed the load to the other shoulder. In a mad dash, we ran out of the room and down the hall. Before we got to the living room, Gram met us. "Where do you think you're going?" she asked, trying desperately to conceal her amusement.

"We saw him! He's coming into the yard!" they screamed.

"Who?" Gram demanded, standing with her fists planted firmly on her plump hips.

"Santa!" they yelled in strange harmony.

I was quiet and didn't want to spoil their fun. There was a knock. My cousins' excitement rose into a frenzy. Gramps opened the door, and there stood an old, tattered, bearded stranger. He said he'd been down at the old Love place to see his kin.

"They left ten years ago," Gramps said.

"I didn't know," the man said.

"Come in and warm yourself," Gramps told him. "Get him some dry clothes," Gramps said to Gram, "and something to eat and a hot drink."

The old traveler unwrapped numerous scarves from his face and removed several hats from his head, sat by the fire, ate, and talked to the grownups. Those dumb kids sat there believing he was Santa Claus. After a little while, Gram hurried us off to bed. The man was gone when we got up on Christmas morning. Gramps' clothes were folded neatly on the daybed in the front hallway, where the man slept. Gram said the man had left us the big bag of toys meant for the Love children. There were carved horses and figures, dolls, handmade jewelry, marbles, and hundreds of other tiny treasures to complete any child's fantasy world.

From the moment most of my cousins had seen the man walking up the lane in the mist, making a sound that may have resembled whispering angels, they had been convinced that he was Santa Claus. I didn't try to tell them any different.

Christmas Shopping

Main Street in downtown Bryan was laden with colorful Christmas lights just after Thanksgiving in the 1960s. As a twelve-year-old, I had developed a superficial interest in Christmas—lush decorations, turkey dinner, and presents under the tree.

"I want to go window shopping," I said to my grandmother.

"Get the catalog," she said.

Disappointed because I wanted to stroll down Main Street and look at window treatments, I went into the bedroom and got the clothing catalog. Carefully I picked up and set down the metal jewelry box when I removed the catalog, which my grandmother kept under the box to protect the dresser surface from scratches.

"I want to go window shopping," I said, taking the book back to the kitchen, where she was rolling out dough for biscuits.

"I hate going to clothing stores," she said, "and being followed around to make sure I don't touch anything."

"Well, you sure can't touch anything but paper in a catalog," I said, trying desperately to make my point.

"What I hate is not being allowed to try something on when all those other women are running back and forth to the fitting room," she said. "If I wanted to try something on—and I don't, because I don't like trying on clothes behind other people—I'd have to buy it first, and I couldn't return it if it didn't fit."

"Some stores will allow us to try on clothes," I said, "but I just want to look around."

"You go breezing in and out of those stores too many times not buying something," she said, "they'll accuse you of stealing."

"But it's Christmas," I whined.

"Christmas doesn't change the law," my grandmother said firmly. "And it doesn't change the way people feel about you. Christmas or not, you won't be able to take one step in a store downtown without somebody breathing loud over your shoulder."

I wasn't getting anywhere with my grandmother, I thought. Maybe my mother would take me window shopping when she and my father came home from work. Stores were open late.

"I'd rather make every stitch of clothes I wear with my own hands and buy the rest from a catalog," my grandmother said, "than spend my money in a place where they go around wiping everything I touch after I leave."

Knowing that our discussion had officially ended when my grandmother turned away, I sat down at the kitchen table and studied the catalog, trying to determine whether or not the pasty model with a plastic hairstyle and cement smile on the cover was a real person or a mannequin.

7

◆

Stepping Out

When the Healer Came to Town

Curious listeners, serious worshippers, and restless children crammed the musty meeting place that night in 1957, when a Houston faith healer had a one-night stand in Bryan.

I was seven or eight, depending on the time of year.

The sound of all those tired feet dragging into the room is still strong in my memory. We found uncomfortable seats on hard pews. I watched oil-lamp flames flicker over sweaty faces.

Mournful voices yelled toward heaven.

Sour notes that hurt my ears rose from the piano.

Raspy throats sang off-key.

I didn't join in, because I didn't know the words and couldn't understand what I heard. I didn't go to church regularly enough to know what they were singing, because my grandmother didn't go. A spirituality that came from some unknown source, much deeper than the good old hypocritical Baptist tradition available on Candy Hill, occupied her soul.

Body heat and humble odor created in that room an atmosphere full of mystery. The despairing souls of my neighbors clung to the edges of their hard benches, waiting to see a miracle. From the crowd, the planted person professing blindness came forward and knelt at a makeshift altar. The healer, adorned in flowing white garments and a high collar, raised his arm. Soft light bounced off the healer's gold wristwatch, as he laid his palm on the pretender.

With a lion's voice, the healer made the rafters rumble: "Be healed!" Through the quake, flakes of plaster fell from the ceiling.

"Amen!" cried the crowd.

Shrieking incomprehensibly until his voice vanished, the healer sprinkled the pretender with water. Worshippers whispered praise. The room fell dead in silence when the lame pretender ascended to human perfection. Emotions ran like a steamy river through the crowd. A woman sitting in a pew near the front slumped forward in a spastic heap. The crowd, on the edge of frenzy, cheered the magic, loosened modest contributions from impoverished pocketbooks, and danced in the aisles.

They bought the big-city healer's blessed fluid, which was nothing more than rainwater in a bottle. They bought the big-city healer's square, wallet-sized sacred prayer cloths, which were no more than cut-up handkerchiefs. They bought the big-city healer's advice to carry the prayer cloth at all times for good luck. Poor Candy Hill folk, shopping for hope, made ideal targets for traveling big-city swindlers and peddlers of superstition.

The Beauty Shop

One Saturday evening in the summer of 1957, I was sitting on the steps of our cottage, where I could see Miss Rosetta's beauty shop across the street as well as I had from the steps of our rent house two doors down. Miss Rosetta had an active beauty business in which she styled her neighbors' hair and sold them perfume, skin cream, shampoo, and hair products, which she kept in a glass case.

The sun was just about to disappear behind the trees at the rear of Miss Rosetta's house beside her little beauty shop. That last golden glow fringed in flame fascinated me, as the pulsating ball drifted lower and lower until all I saw was a bright halo around Miss Rosetta's house.

My eight-year-old heart saddened. The sun was gone. I knew it wasn't really gone. When I was five, my cousin Joyce had told me the sun was shining on someone else when it wasn't shining on me.

The single light bulb by the front door of Miss Rosetta's beauty shop burned as she finished her last customer for the day. The dim light reflected off a big glass thermometer and a metal RC Cola sign in the shape of a soda-bottle cap, both attached to the side wall of the aging frame building.

I sat on our porch wondering who was sitting in Miss Rosetta's leather beauty chair and wishing I was the one having my hair done up in curls. Every time I asked for a hair press and curls, Miss Rosetta told me I didn't need a press. My grandmother said I played so hard Saturday morning that curls would be full of dirt by Saturday night. Well, that wasn't so bad, since my best friend Doris had been told the same thing; and I knew that, given the chance, she would be at school Monday morning slinging her greasy hair in my face and laughing at me, still in braids.

The smell of burning hair had been strong all morning and after-noon. The next day, after all, would be the first Sunday of the month. Women who never wore curls paid Miss Rosetta to anoint their heads with Royal Crown Hair Pomade and fry fresh shiny curls into their hair for church. Usually she didn't work at night. "I'm too old to work by anything but God's light," I remembered hearing her say, while I imagined the aging beautician's glasses down low on her nose while she sweated and wrestled with resistant hair.

On summer nights, Miss Rosetta sat on her screened-in front porch eating vanilla ice cream. She kept a pantry of goodies, ice cream, six-cent RC Colas, five-cent candy bars, Popsicles, Dixie Cups, penny cookies, loaves of bread, and potato chips, which she sold to her neighbors. I had seen every one of Miss Rosetta's customers coming and going that day except the one still in the beauty shop. Who could it be getting their hair styled and keeping Miss Rosetta in the shop this late?

Sunny Nash standing in front of her family's cottage on Easter Sunday, 1958.

My mother, who was always reading to me out of *National Geographic,* once read that hair was created to help skin and skull protect the brain in extreme temperatures. She said that hair styling—demonstrated in Egyptian and other African art, as well as Eastern, Middle Eastern, Asian, Native American, Greek, and European drawings, etchings, paintings, statues, figurines, and coins—dates back about four thousand years. Ancient African societies communicated tribal affiliation, social position, age, and marital status with hairstyles.

By the time she started explaining about hair styling during slavery, I was ready to go out and play, but she wouldn't let me. "Sit down and be quiet," she said. "You need to know this stuff. During slavery, transplanted Africans lost their customs and adopted American prejudices toward light skin and fine hair. After slavery, light-skinned black people from Louisiana segregated themselves from their own family.

Lots of them passed themselves off as other races so they could get better treatment, education, and opportunity."

"What happened to them if they were found out?" I asked.

"Killed," she said.

"A teacher was measuring everybody's braids against Lovie Level's braids one day," I said.

"You know that's wrong, don't you?" she asked.

"Yeah."

"Yes," she corrected me.

"Lovie got mad because my braid was longer than hers."

"There are beautiful people in this world who have hair that looks like a curly swimming cap and they're the color of night," my mother said. "Don't let anyone measure your hair or anything else on you like that again."

My mother's hair lesson went on. Unable to realize their good looks while living in subhuman conditions, African people in America and Europe fell victim to a beauty standard so narrow that few humans—black or white, living or dead—can squeeze into it. The only hair-grooming aid for many African-American women was a head-rag to cover what they had been taught to regard with shame.

Then came the hot comb! But long before the hot comb was available to African-American women, it was used by kinky-haired Caucasian-American women of European descent, who hid in their homes and beauty shops for decades, silently pressing their hair. It wasn't until the 1920s, my mother said, that Madam C. J. Walker modified the European hot comb and gave women of color styling freedom to remove their head-rags and achieve the same hairstyles as their kinky-haired Caucasian-American cousins. Throughout the 1940s, hot irons were the only commercial hair straighteners. African-American men invented a home-made chemical relaxing concoction they called "the conk," used by male entertainers in the days when natural hair was still a public disgrace. Chemical straighteners came onto the U.S. market in the 1950s, but Miss Rosetta said her training didn't go that far.

I stared at the beauty shop door, trying to guess who would come out. The light went out at the laundry next to Miss Rosetta's shop. The ladies there, who washed and ironed for rich people all over town, had poured out their tubs of suds and put away their boards for the evening and were walking home.

Wealthy women with stockinged legs, slim skirts, and bouffant hair drove fancy cars to the laundry all day, dropping off their husbands' soiled white shirts, their grimy bed linens and slimy towels. I went over one day to take a look when I heard the laundry ladies laughing at a heap of things they'd poured out on the ground. "Get a club!" someone yelled. "It's alive!"

"Good evening, Miss Willie," I said as one of the laundry ladies passed our house. The streetlamp came on at the corner. It sure was taking Miss Rosetta a long time. Finally I heard the rusty door-hinges squeal. Oh, no—Doris!

There Goes the Beef

I stared enviously at the black-and-white photograph of a model in a *True Confessions* makeup advertisement. Heavy pencil lined her drooping eyelids. Her eyebrows were arched high in a thin line. Long fake lashes framed her eyes. Pouting lips dominated her face. Her straw-like hair flipped at the ends.

I bet she eats her steaks rare, I thought.

The summer of 1960, when I turned eleven, I ruined my eyebrows with a pair of tweezers trying to make them look like the model's. That was also the summer when I tried to get my first taste of a steak cooked rare. Although roast beef was a regular dish in our house, it wasn't until my father moved in with us that we had steaks more frequently. Steaks were rare on Candy Hill. Most people had meals featuring nineteen-cent-a-pound chicken from Food Town or ox tails or various external and internal pig parts from Humpty-Dumpty Food Market.

I thought steaks were special because a cow was higher from the ground than a chicken or a hog. And a cow never wallowed in a muddy hole and ate a more discriminating diet than insects, table scraps, or slop. I'd seen steaks in magazines prepared rare, oozing blood and lying on a platter surrounded by potatoes and corn on the cob. On television and in movies, glamorous, diamond-studded people, with long cigarette-holders and smoke swirling in little circles about their faces, ordered their steaks rare in restaurants.

That summer, my grandmother and I were visiting relatives who were cooking meat and roasting ears of corns on an outdoor grill. I bragged to my cousins that I ate my steaks rare. To their amazement, when I thought none of the grownups was looking, I forked a steak that was hardly cooked on one side. I should have known better, because my grandmother was always looking, even when she didn't seem to be looking. Still annoyed but somewhat amused by the new look about my eyes—one eyebrow higher and thinner than the other— she marched over to our little group and grabbed my plate. "You can't eat raw meat!"

"It's not raw," I explained. "It's rare."

My grandmother forked the steak and slapped it back on the grill. The hot coals sizzled as blood from the meat dripped through the grate. "Rare is raw! You want to get sick?"

"No." I watched the red edges of the meat turn crispy brown.

"Things live in raw meat." She turned the steak over to the other side. "Things that are just waiting to get into your stomach and multiply. You cook the meat to kill those things."

Heat extracted blood, fat, and other moisture from the meat. Each drop hissed and whined in the fire. When the agony ended and the steak was well done, my grandmother put it back on my plate.

"No, thank you," I said, imagining things I couldn't see tunneling through the meat. "I'll just have some corn."

The Halloween Scare

My mother hadn't been the same since that set of encyclopedias and reference books came into our house in the fall of 1961.

I'd never seen anyone who wasn't doing homework spend that much time in a book. She said that people at universities were always in books trying to prove what they thought by finding something similar that someone else had written. Honestly, I thought my mother's curiosity would wear off eventually and we'd start watching television at night and having dinner on time again.

Her curiosity, however, didn't wear off. In fact, it got worse! Obsessed with what seemed to me the tiniest bits of trivia from the past as well as the present, she started buying newspapers every day instead of every other day. Although she never asked me any questions, I knew she expected me to read those stories about the Cold War, the conflict in Southeast Asia, and the civil rights movement. Beginning in the sixth grade, every night after my homework, I sat down with the newspaper and read all of the headlines and at least the first couple of sentences of each story, just in case she asked me something.

My mother's involvement in books got so intense that it began to affect our family. We never watched television anymore after dinner. My father enrolled in night school; and, although she denied it, my grandmother was sneaking around reading most of the day when she was home alone.

"Your grandmother won't let you catch her studying or reading," my mother had told me, "because she wants everyone to think she already knows it all."

One day in late October, I walked home from school, trying to figure a way to get out of dressing up in some stupid costume my mother brought home from Woolworth's and going door-to-door begging for candy I'd never eat. When I got home, the house was more than quiet. The television was dark. Nothing boiled or fried on the stove. A strange hush hovered over the whole place. I put my school-books on top of the bookcase. The "H" encyclopedia was missing from the shelf below. I tiptoed through the living room toward the kitchen and saw my grandmother hunkered down at the kitchen table buried in the book. Eyes in back of her head made her slam the book shut and turn suddenly.

"Did you know that Halloween was originally a festival for the dead?" my grandmother shouted, trying to conceal her excitement. "People believed witches and warlocks flew around on that night. They built bonfires to ward off ghosts and goblins and demons and spirits. I knew that evil day was uncivilized heathen worship! You will not be celebrating Halloween in this house again!"

Her eyes were twinkling when she rushed past me and put the book back. For the first time, I fully appreciated the power of the information in my mother's reference books.

A Neighborhood Institution

There was no mistaking that smell, floating like a huge aromatic cloud over West Bryan, making everyone's mouth water! It was the smell of hamburgers—real hamburgers. Round, ground meat patties frying on a greasy grill that was well-seasoned with charred drippings, salt, pepper, and tiny brown flecks of toasted onion.

In the 1950s and 1960s, no pre-cooked, pre-packaged fast foods were being hauled into Bryan, Texas, in the backs of refrigerated trucks. All of the food, grown in local gardens or on nearby farms, was pre-pared from scratch right on the premises by the hands of neighbor-hood folks who generally owned the establishments and knew their regular customers by name.

The aroma of hamburgers grew stronger, the closer I got to Little-ton's Snack Bar on West Nineteenth Street, now West Martin Luther

King. Walking home from football and basketball games or other school activities in the evening or on Saturdays, Kemp High School students stopped at Littleton's to eat and socialize on the wooden picnic benches beside the tiny building, which was only large enough to hold a kitchen.

Because it was within walking distance of the campus, Littleton's monopolized the Kemp school lunch business. Across the street from the Kemp campus, Scott's Place served balanced soul-food lunches and dinners of steak, pork, and chicken; vegetables and greens cooked with ham-hocks; candied yams, mashed potatoes, and gravy; and fresh-fruit cobblers. Teachers and other adults ate at Scott's, but students found it too much like eating at home. With Mrs. Scott running the place, telling us where to sit, what to eat, behave yourself, and be quiet, we might as well have been at home with our own mothers. Littleton's was our place.

"Hello, honey," said a smiling Mrs. Littleton, leaning down to the little window to take my order. Her white uniform glowed in the sun. Her long hair, pulled back in a bun, was tucked under a shimmery hairnet. "What can I fix for you today?"

"A hamburger with everything," I said. "French fries and a cherry cola float."

"That'll be fifty cents," she said.

I carefully counted out twenty-five cents for the hamburger, ten cents for the fries, and another fifteen cents for the float, and placed it on the counter. With the tip of her apron, Mrs. Littleton raked the coins into their proper place in the cash drawer. I never saw her touch money with her bare hands. Standing on my toes, I watched her take a fresh meat patty from the refrigerator, touching only the paper liner around the meat with her hands. She slapped my meat on the grill, and its smoke rose through the vent over the stove and joined the aromatic cloud that hung overhead.

Until folks began to get their pleasure from gimmicks and flashy wrappers in the late 1960s, Littleton's Snack Bar was a neighborhood institution.

My Grandmother's Little White Gloves

Our clothesline was alive with white gloves making piano-playing motions in a breeze. From my swing, I watched my grandmother wash and hang the tiny garments to dry.

My grandmother owned hundreds of white gloves and never went out in public without wearing a pair. Opening her Christmas, birthday, or Mother's Day presents, she never wanted to be surprised. On any gift-giving occasion, everyone in the family knew that white gloves would please her better than silk scarves or satin lingerie or expensive perfume. One birthday, an out-of-town daughter sent her a wristwatch. I'd never seen such disappointment as when she opened the box and saw the slender gold-mesh band and diamond face. I was glad she hated the watch, because, when I was in seventh grade, she let me wear it on special occasions.

Some of my grandmother's gloves, sent to her from other countries by family members serving in the military, were made of the softest woven fabrics, with fine stitching around each finger part and double stitching on the hand parts. Some of the gloves were handcrafted, fancily embroidered, or cut from elegant lace that wound into intricate spidery patterns. And at least one special pair had been crocheted of ivory yarn so silky and delicate that the gloves could be made to fit into a thimble.

Collecting little white gloves was not a hobby with my grandmother. In fact, she seldom went anywhere without wearing gloves. Her nagging obsession with cleanliness, and in particular with clean hands, required gloves for all outings. To her, of course, this obsession with clean hands—an anxiety unusual in the early 1960s, when air, water, food, and people were considered relatively safe—was not a phobia. It was ordinary behavior. Still, the condition prevented her from having unprotected contact with anything that people outside our household had also touched. Public doorknobs, handles, stair rails, elevator buttons, telephones, and merchandise in stores were all off-limits to that germ-conscious woman, although I don't know if I ever heard her use the word *germ* to explain her conduct.

Especially repulsive to her was unprotected handshaking. After a handshake, she explained to me once, you've now touched everything that person has touched. "You know the shaking hand is the one people use in the bathroom, and most people do not wash after every flush," I'd heard her say many times.

My grandmother's obsession with clean hands also led her to loathe money. If money ever touched her exposed skin, she'd spend several minutes scrubbing her fingers and palms raw with a brush afterwards. When I was a little girl, it didn't seem fair to me that this woman who loathed touching money always seemed to have some in her possession.

One day, she took her wallet from her purse, stretched it open, and dumped money out on the table. Then she picked through the bills with tweezers and made her selection. With tweezers—her normal way of handling of money until a hospital-worker friend brought her some surgical gloves—she held a dollar by its limp corner. I must have been looking at her very oddly as she tweezed the money. "This dollar must have been through a thousand hands. I don't want to touch it," she said. "There's nothing filthier on earth."

I stared at the dangling dollar bill and imagined varieties of invisible organisms oozing from its filthy cracks, sliding around on the slimy surface, and dripping from it. "Take it," my grandmother said. She wouldn't touch that dollar with her own bare hands, but she expected me to take it to the store. "Looks like somebody used this dollar to blow their nose and then wiped up the bathroom floor with it," she said. "And it smells like it, too." Until I heard that graphic description, I'd never had a problem touching money.

"Go on and take it," she said, shaking the dollar at me. "And hurry back from the store." Disgusted with money for the first time in my life, I took the wilted paper between the tips of thumb and index finger, pulled my blouse pocket open and dropped the money inside.

From my swing, I watched my grandmother lather smudges and grime from the tips of her gloves. Making tiny circular motions on the fabric, her fingers gently eased out the more stubborn dark stains. After rinsing the gloves in plain water, she dropped them in bleach to disinfect and whiten. Finally the gloves hit the bluing bucket for a final rinse and came out glowing.

I jumped off the swing and walked over to the clothesline. "Why do you have to wear gloves when you go out?" I asked.

"Do you see how dirty the water is?" She took another glove from the rinse bucket. A tiny network of veins rose on the back of her hand when she squeezed the bluing water out of the fabric.

"Yes."

"That should tell you my reasons for wearing gloves." She pinned the glove on the line. "Some of these gloves have been to a bank, a train station, and department stores in other states."

"Well, I hope you don't think I'm going to wear gloves everywhere I go," I said.

"That's up to you," she said. "You have to eat with your hands, I don't."

8

◆

Influences

Little Pieces of Freedom

I decided to wait on the porch for the postman that crisp sunny Saturday morning. The cool dry air reminded me of Denver, where I'd spent the previous summer.

Cartoons blared through the open living room window. I didn't care about missing their zany make-believe antics, which no longer amused me. And the commercials were of no use, since my mother had stopped buying the breakfast cereals they advertised, because, she said, all that sugar made me act funny. Besides, by the time I was eleven years old, I was more concerned about my own future than the trouble Tweetie Bird faced outside his cage or whether Sweet'pea was Olive Oyl's illegitimate child.

My summer vacation in Denver, where I had felt free for the first time in my life, had changed me. I had sat in the front of a bus, sipped a chocolate shake at a soda fountain, ate a hamburger inside a restaurant, went through the same door as everyone else to a movie, and tried on a dress in a department store. Exposure to seemingly innocent privileges had affected me deeply and frightened me to the core. I worried privately that I could no longer accept rear entrances, back seats, inferior quality, and the other scraps of hand-me-down, second-hand living in Bryan. But being a child, what could I do?

I sat down on our porch step and peered up the street, looking for the postman. Getting mail had always excited me, even if the letters didn't have my name on them. It was amazing to me that an envelope could travel to us on Candy Hill from Denver, where my Aunt Clara lived; or Cleveland, where my Aunt Leslie lived; or New York or California, where my uncles lived; or Germany, where my cousin was stationed in the military.

By 1961, we had a telephone that rang infrequently. I never expected to take a call from any of my few Candy Hill friends who had telephones. My grandmother insisted that the instrument be used only in emergencies. Although she received occasional calls from relatives in other towns, she never called them. "Long-distance costs too much," she said. "And you say things on the phone that you can't take back. It's better to write. If you don't like what you said, you can always tear it up and start over."

I stood up when I saw the postman carrying the huge leather satchel on his shoulder, his crisp blue uniform slightly moist at the armpits. My heart jumped when he toiled toward our house. Without breaking his stride, he put the mail in my outstretched palm, nodded, and kept walking. On top of the stack was a letter for me! Between vacations from Candy Hill, letters from far-away places represented little pieces of freedom.

Door=to=Door Sales

On Tuesdays, elderly Mr. Watkins came to Candy Hill in his blue Chevy and brought goods to show to my somewhat rude but unpretentious grandmother. She preferred his ill-fitting matronly line of light cotton print dresses to the slightly nicer ones she was not allowed to try on downtown. Also Mr. Watkins offered, and my grandmother regularly purchased, thick opaque stockings and thick-soled old-lady shoes, all of which she wore every day. For special occasions, she had fine silks, nylons, and satin, which my mother bought and brought home to her from Lester's on Main Street.

"Watkins, everything you have to sell is too ugly to be buried in," I once heard my grandmother tell him. "Don't you have anything but these mammy-made housecoats?"

"Well, Edna, when y'all get a ride to town to shop for what you want," Mr. Watkins would say, "y'all won't need me to come 'round showing you nothing no more, now, will y'all?"

Transportation was just one reason poor people stayed away from the marketplaces in the 1950s. In rural areas and small towns as well, family-owned cars were still rare among low-income families. Only in the largest cities could a person expect to find reliable public transportation. In Bryan, during the 1950s, however, there were a few city buses. These noisy, slow-moving, open-air buses rocked side-to-side north and south on Texas Avenue, connecting maids to their jobs in well-to-do College Station households and custodial workers to the college, which most North Bryan residents called Texas A&M.

"You can almost get where you're going faster if you walk," riders complained, "rather than ride the bus."

Spending a much higher percentage of their income on goods than those with more money, poor people regularly bought clothes from the trunks of cars and food from the backs of trucks. Settling for the unattractive and inferior grades, people with limited resources traditionally have paid more for products than the products were worth in other markets.

My grandmother was talking with Miss Odessa and hanging clothes on the line in the backyard. Our dog, Old Sally, had started barking when Miss Odessa's car rolled up and stopped at the side of our house. I couldn't tell if she was getting used to her car or not. She still didn't drive it fast enough for the gears to change. Old Sally, straining against her chain, wasn't friendly to anyone, but she hated Miss Odessa more than anyone except Mrs. Blue, who hadn't come by since Old Sally bit her. My grandmother said Old Sally probably hated the women's perfume. My mother had a theory, too. Old Sally's irritation with the women was caused by their jangling jewelry. I insisted that Old Sally was bothered by the bright colors the women wore. But my grandmother said dogs couldn't tell the difference between bright and dull colors.

"May as well buy cheap clothes from Mr. Watkins," I overheard my grandmother say to Miss Odessa. "Can't try on those high-priced clothes downtown. Everybody scared some black is going to rub off of you in the clothes and end up on some of them," she laughed.

"They still don't seem to know that ain't how people stay white," said Miss Odessa, who was about the color of the inside of a buttery pound cake. "You born that way."

Miss Odessa had no color to rub off, I thought.

"And if you buy something you like and find out the fit is bad when you get it home, you can't take it back and get your money," my grandmother said to Miss Odessa. "You're broke and stuck with something that you'll have to give away. May as well buy cheap clothes from Mr. Watkins."

"How can poor folks control their own lives when they let some outsider like Watkins come in and have control of their clothes, food, water, air we breathe, and even our dreams?" my mother commented more than once.

"And don't forget about beer," my grandmother added. "People get rich off of selling beer."

"You think we can strut up to city hall and apply for a beer license?" my mother asked.

"You can strut up there and apply for one," my grandmother said, "but you sure won't get it. Those folks downtown keep us out of all the money-making. That's how they keep their feet on our necks! Keep us fighting one another for leftovers and hand-me-downs. Keep us begging! Keep us depending on them for scraps!"

"I know you're right." A deep sadness settled around my mother's eyes as she went about the task of creating a home for us out of nothing and trying to make someone useful out of me.

I was sitting in the living room doing homework when Mr. Watkins, holding a suitcase, knocked on the screen door. "Edna home?" he asked, peering through the screen wire.

"I'll see," I said, going to the back door and calling her.

My grandmother walked in through the kitchen door. She and Mr. Watkins exchanged grunted greetings while he opened his suitcase of plain cotton dresses and chunky shoes. When he saw Miss Odessa, with her jangling jewelry, perfectly applied gaudy makeup, nylon stockings, yellow silk dress, and fluttering eyelashes, and smelled her sweet-smelling perfume, he bolted back to his car like he'd seen a ghost! He returned with another case.

"Odessa, I thought I'd missed my best customer this week," Mr. Watkins said, grinning. "You haven't been home." He opened the case and presented things I was sure would anger Old Sally—perfumes, jewelry, glittery hair combs, fluffy red blouses, and shiny patent-leather shoes.

"I've been getting around," Miss Odessa said, looking at Mr. Watkins's things with disinterest. "At the five-and-dime, I can get more things for a lot cheaper than you selling them."

"Well, Odessa, when y'all get a ride to town to shop," Mr. Watkins said, "y'all won't need me no more."

Television Housewives

In 1961, one of my eleven-year-old friends told me she wanted to be a housewife when she grew up.

"Like Beaver Cleaver's mom?" I asked.

"Yes," she insisted. "Like June!"

"And sit around all day dressed up?" I asked. "With your hair in tight little frizzy curls like Lucy and Ethel?"

"Yes, a housewife!" she said. "Like Harriet Nelson!"

"Waiting for Ozzie to come home?" I asked.

"You ever see Harriet wash dishes?" she asked. "Or Donna Reed? They throw away the plates when they get dirty. Housewives don't do dishes or laundry or floors. Some even have maids."

I was confused walking home. That housewife business didn't sound like anything I wanted to do. Who in their right mind would want to sit around the house all day, tossing dirty plates in the trash and waiting for Ozzie to come home?

My grandmother was sweeping the porch when I got home. She wasn't dressed up. But, as usual, her crisp white apron covered a wrinkle-free cotton print dress; her stockings were gartered below the knee; her hair was center-parted; and a long, neat braid lay on each shoulder. Laundry waved on the clothesline by the side of the house. The aroma of fresh pound cake was strong.

"Are you a housewife?" I asked, walking into the yard.

"Yes," she said. "A maid who doesn't get paid."

"Georgia said that's what she's going to be," I said.

"Georgia wants to be a maid?" my grandmother asked.

"No, a housewife!"

"Well, her chances of being a maid are better!" she said. "Because, until you get old like me and have to help out with your grandchildren, you will probably have to work for somebody else, whether you have a husband or not."

I knew my grandmother was right. There was not one young housewife on Candy Hill, but there were plenty of young maids.

"I don't want to be a housewife or a maid," I said. "I want to be a boss, like a man, so I can make a lot of money."

"First of all, you don't know any men who are bosses." She breathed deeply. "Second, you think earning a lot of money will make you more important than a housewife?"

Feeling myself starting to sweat, I'd trapped myself. Afraid to answer, I swallowed hard. "No," I whispered.

"Well, it won't!" she scolded. "I don't care what you do for a living or how much money you make," she said, "you will sleep with your eyes closed and open your mouth to eat just like all the other men and women on earth, whether they are maids, housewives, or bosses!"

Television Cowboys

I stared at the black-and-white television picture of Marshal Matt Dillon's long pasty face frowning in the bright sunshine. Or was he smiling? It was hard to tell. With his gunbelt slung low on his board-flat hips, the marshal's booted feet strolled from the jail across Dodge City's main dirt road to the saloon, where all the cowboys hung out, drank liquor straight from the bottle, and shot each other sometimes for no reason. Whining about Doc's bad attitude, Chester hobbled along not far behind the marshal. This 1960s' washed-out television portrayal of the Old West didn't intrigue me as much as bother me, making me uneasy with myself and my world. I was only twelve years old, but I sensed there was something missing from the story, something wrong about the way it was spread out so neatly before me.

Those make-believe images of busty Miss Kitty, smiling from one side of her mouth, irritated me like they never had before. Busy serving up sarcastic humor with every glass of good cheer she poured, Miss Kitty's long black eyelashes stood apart like frog's toes. No longer hearing what she said, I stared at the contrast between the prominent round mole beside her mouth and the porcelain quality of her very pale face.

"You're sitting too close to the television." My grandmother's voice startled me. When I turned around, she was looking into the living room at me from the kitchen. "They say sitting that close will ruin your eyes."

I pushed up my heavy glasses and went to the kitchen. "Where are the black cowboys?"

"The first black cowboys were slaves on horses," she said.

"Slaves!" I shouted. "Slaves were cowboys?"

"Breaking horses and herding cattle across the country to market was work," she said impatiently, as if I should have known that. "Who do you think did the work during slavery times?"

"But there are no black cowboys on television," I said.

"Because somebody put something on television so they could sell their soap and cigarettes doesn't make it real," she said.

I left the kitchen, ashamed that I had learned the history of the American West from the imaginations of Hollywood producers whose wandering characters played out-of-tune guitars, sang to their horses, outdrew each other at high noon, ate trail dust, and rode off into the sunset but left the hard work to real cowboys.

Everything That Makes You Laugh Isn't Funny

"Turn off that television!" My mother stormed into the living room, yelling in the angriest voice her sweet disposition could muster, nearly jarring me off the couch. "I won't have you watching *Amos and Andy*! And filling your head with nonsense! You get enough nonsense from these Candy Hill streets!"

Too stunned to move, I'm sure my mouth was hanging open.

"Close your mouth," she snapped. "If I catch you watching those ignorant, shuffling, yassah-boss fools again, I'll get rid of the television and you can read all the time."

My soft-spoken, gentle mother seldom raised her voice to me or anyone. Although I never heard her argue, she sometimes allowed me some debate about inconsequential decisions—what to wear to school, how I should wear my hair, what to eat for breakfast, or when to go to bed. Sometimes, if I presented my points strongly enough, she'd even let me win.

"You already know how to act stupid," she yelled. "I've seen you and your little friends do that many times—making ugly faces at each other, stretching your mouths open, crossing your eyes, walking like you're crippled, changing your voice, singing off-key, dancing a jig and kicking up dirt, and scratching your behinds like monkeys. All that stuff makes you look stupid!"

She was right. And the stupider it looked, the more we did it, and the harder we laughed.

"Its hard enough teaching you to speak correctly, without having Kingfish, Lightning, and Andy bursting every verb in and out of the book," she said hotly. "Don't they make you ashamed?"

"Yeah," I said softly, lying, not thinking of Amos and Andy in harmful terms. I wanted to watch them because they made me laugh; and, in the 1950s and 1960s, Amos and Andy were the only black people on television, except for Jack Benny's butler, Rochester.

"Yes," she corrected me. "Everything that makes you laugh isn't funny! But as long as everyone seems to be having a good time, people keep accepting stupidity and pain as funny, without even thinking about it. Understand?"

"Yes," I said, dropping my head.

"The only way for some folk to survive," she said, "is to hide behind a big wide grin so no one sees how it hurts to be kicked, stomped, raped, pushed to the back, laughed at, and worse. And the laws of these United States of America still allow it! Well, things are going to change. And when they do, you're going to do more with your life than be here just for someone else's use or their pleasure or their amusement!"

Without a word, I got up and turned off the television.

Deaf Woman from Baltimore

Waldine was married. Waldine was *really* married! Waldine was really married to Ralph, a military man stationed at Bryan Air Force Base. A deaf woman, Waldine was from up north—Baltimore, Maryland, I think. I can't remember exactly. That was about 1956 or 1957, and I was only six or seven years old when I knew her.

Living in a silent world, Waldine fascinated me. Her days were so different from mine, which were filled with sounds I didn't want to hear and sometimes with just plain noise. Waldine said she didn't want to hear all that stuff, anyway. She said she wouldn't do it to herself, even if doctors could operate on her ears, fix them, and allow her to hear. When Waldine didn't want to be bothered with the activities around her, she simply looked away, retreating peacefully into silence.

Oh, how I envied that.

Waldine could read lips better than most folks could hear. One afternoon, she and I were walking from the store. She read Sugar's lips from across the street and told me everything he said. Didn't miss a word. Sugar was an old man who lived in the neighborhood. He was working in his garden that day and cursing out the birds as they swooped down and picked the blossoms from his tomato plants.

Oh, yeah, Waldine could talk, too. Her words, however, were so labored that speech seemed painful for her. Most Candy Hill folks didn't have the patience to listen to her. They saw her as just another neighborhood freak, much like Joe the dwarf who lived down the trail from the store, or the old bald-headed lady who lived across from the graveyard, or the boy with the club foot, or the web-fingered girl, or the man who whistled all the time, or the woman who spoke every word in rhyme.

Listening for hours, until my own throat hurt, I loved hearing about the places Waldine and Ralph had been. She said she was raised in a foster home because no one wanted her, not even her own parents, who left her to die in a garbage can. Then she had to explain to me what a foster home was, since I'd never heard of such a home.

One night, Waldine said, her foster brother Tod put the needle down on a record in his room. He turned to her and said, "We have to work out this rhythm thing. You can't dance without rhythm."

Waldine watched Tod's hands clapping out the beat. He picked up her hands and clapped them for her. "I can't imagine what music sounds like," she said with her fingers. "This is stupid. Get a real date, Tod."

Tod said, "No! Please try one more time."

"You feel sorry for me," she told him. "That's why you're doing this."

She said he led her to the floor, where they laid down. He flattened her palms on the floor. "Feel it?" he asked. "Little Richard."

She said she felt the floor bumping under her hands.

"Sing," Tod said. "'Tutti Frutti.'"

Waldine said she sang "Tutti Frutti" with Tod over and over again, until she had memorized all the words and still wondered what a Little Richard was and what "Tutti Frutti" meant. Then she said she felt something else on the floor—their foster mother, Mrs. Ballinger, stomping into the room.

"I was just trying to help her feel the music," Tod said.

"No way for a dummy to know music," Mrs. Ballinger yelled. Tod fingered what the woman said for Waldine, like he did most times when he thought someone was speaking too fast for her to read their lips. "Cut out that finger talk and go to bed, Tod!" Mrs. Ballinger scolded.

The woman shoved Waldine to her room and locked the door from the outside. Waldine didn't sleep that night. The next morning, Mrs. Ballinger unlocked the door after the other children had gone to school. She yanked a pillowcase off the bed and stuffed Waldine's things into it. Pushing the bundle into the girl's hands, Mrs. Ballinger shoved her all the way to the back door of the house, where Mr. Ballinger was waiting.

"Go with him," Mrs. Ballinger said. "I want you gone."

Standing by the back door, Mrs. Ballinger pushed Waldine toward Mr. Ballinger and screamed, "Go on!"

Waldine said her feet dug into the rug.

"What's wrong with you?" Mrs. Ballinger demanded.

Waldine said she dropped her bundle, grabbed her breasts, one in each hand, and squeezed. Then she pointed at Mr. Ballinger. Mrs. Ballinger looked at her husband suspiciously and told Waldine to wait outside.

Waldine told me that she didn't want to go with Mr. Ballinger, because he was a dirty old man. I asked her if a dirty old man was anything like Mr. Jake, who worked on the outhouse crew? Waldine said, not the kind of dirty that needs washing. The Mr. Hines kind of dirty, looking under little girls' dresses and touching them where he shouldn't. It didn't take long for people to learn about Mr. Hines. Waldine had only been living on Candy Hill for a short time, and she knew about him.

Oh, I uttered, thinking that Mrs. Hines was the meanest woman I'd ever known. Her face had creases that can only come from being mean. Folds of rough skin draped over the upper parts of her yellowed eyes. Her solidified cheeks looked like she was hiding rocks in her mouth. All the neighborhood children were warned to stay away from that house! Mr. Hines would feel on you if you were a girl, and Mrs. Hines would kill you, boy or girl.

Mr. Hines never felt on me, maybe because I didn't have anything to feel yet. He felt on Jewel. At least, she said he did. I don't know. But she's the only one who said anything. I do remember Mr. Hines chasing us around the yard with an old, dried-up rooster head from a dead member of the flock he raised in the backyard. Because we knew he could never catch us, we loved playing in that yard and running from Mr. Hines.

I don't remember Mrs. Hines ever killing anyone, but I do remember seeing her in their front yard one morning about dawn, cutting down the mulberry tree that all the kids loved. I saw her through the window with the sun rising in a misty sky behind her. And she was chopping and grunting!

Chopping and grunting!

Chopping and grunting!

Chopping and grunting until that friendly neighborhood tree was laying dead, halfway in the street.

Waldine told me that one night when she was folding clothes, Mr. Ballinger sneaked up behind her and grabbed her breasts. She threw hot sheets from the gas dryer on him. She said that old fool tried to laugh it off, pulling the sheets off and backing out of the laundry room. She never told this to Mrs. Ballinger. Waldine told me she was washing dishes one night, and Mr. Ballinger sneaked up and grabbed her behind. She said she dashed hot greasy dishwater in his face. He tried to laugh that off, too. She never told this to Mrs. Ballinger. Waldine told me Mr. Ballinger picked the lock on the bathroom door while she was in the tub. He dove into her bath water, head first. She caught his face between her knees, wrapped her legs around his neck, and held his head under the water, while he sloshed out nearly all her bubble bath. Gasping, he freed himself and crawled toward the door. She said he wasn't laughing that time. Waldine never told this to Mrs. Ballinger, either.

Picking up her bundle and walking out, Waldine knew she didn't want another foster family. Turning sixteen in a week, she'd be free to do whatever she wanted.

I asked Waldine what she did after that.

She said she got a job in a titty bar in Baltimore, met Ralph while dancing nude on a table, got married, traveled all over the world, and finally met a nosy little girl in Texas.

"How'd you hear the music to dance?" I asked.

"It was so loud, the floor vibrated," she said.

"Waldine, what's a titty bar?" I asked.

"Something you don't need to know about yet," she said, laughing.

What a Woman Needs to Know

I knew it had to be serious if my mother was calling me a woman.

"There's been talk about strange men coming to Candy Hill offering little girls money to go with them," she said.

I wasn't about to go anywhere with any strange man or woman, whether I knew them or not. How could I tell my mother that my grandmother had already told me about perverted people and who, in particular, to watch.

"Are you listening?" my mother asked.

"Yes," I said, thinking about the day my classmate Sharon and I were walking home from school. A lot bigger than I was, taller and heavier, Sharon could have passed for fourteen, although we were both eleven years old that spring of 1961. She lived out on the Graveyard Line past Candy Hill, and some days she walked past my house on her way home. Both rough neighborhoods turned children into premature adults before they reached puberty.

Near my house, a man drove a blue car down the middle of narrow, gravel Henderson Street, slowed, and called, "Hey!" Glancing at him, Sharon and I moved far into the drainage ditch away from his car and walked a little faster.

"Hey, you little whores!" he yelled again, waving some dollar bills out the car window, as his speed picked up to match ours. "I'm talking to y'all! Can't the dummies hear?" More shocked than afraid, Sharon and I gave each other the eye at the same magical, volatile, dangerous moment.

"I bet your wife doesn't know you're down here," Sharon said, stepping toward the car, just out of reach.

"Get in," he said. "I'll give you some money."

"How much?" she asked, keeping his attention off me.

"More than you ever had," he said, his blue eyes reflecting the sun like pools of cold water.

I eased up to the door and grabbed the bills from his relaxed fist. "And more than you got," I shouted.

"Give me back my money," he said, getting out of the car.

Yelling two-foot long obscenities at him, we dropped our books, picked up rocks, pelted his body and face.

Wilma and Billie Jean's father, Mr. Willie Robinson, who worked nights, ran out of his house wearing only his boxer shorts. "What's going on out here?" he yelled, rubbing sleepy eyes.

Throwing rocks, Sharon and I chased the stranger into his car. Mr. Robinson chuckled and went back in his house after the man drove away. Before the stranger was out of sight, I had counted the ten dollars and handed Sharon five of it.

"If anybody bothers you," my mother said, "make as much noise as possible. Defend yourself with whatever you can get your hands on. Then run. Don't take money from anyone! Understand?"

9

◆

Neighbors

Out of Sight

One Saturday morning when I was four years old, I turned on our battery radio and watched the glow of the clear glass tubes, coming to life and readying themselves for operation. When I switched the dial, searching for a station, the radio whined until I reached the pecking, high-pitched squeals and spirited narration of the *Woody Woodpecker Show.*

Television hadn't been around long enough to earn the nickname "TV." Advertisers, producers, programmers, old folks, unbelievers, and other holdouts speculated that fascination with the big tube would pass. No one honestly entertained the idea that people would grow lazy enough to sit around all day watching someone else live in a little box.

So, for some time, radio got the loyalty, the best shows, and the commercial dollars. Later, in the middle 1950s, TV advertisers began tapping adult markets with soap and cigarettes, and children's markets during Saturday cartoons with commercials for breakfast cereals loaded with sugar and other juvenile junk that my mother wouldn't buy for me, no matter how hard I begged: "Oh, please, I'll wash all the dishes in the world and clean every kid's bedroom in town, including mine, if you buy me that plastic thing with the red string that stretches around the end and it flies!"

In the middle of Woody's cackling, I thought I heard a baby crying, but no one was in the house but me. It wasn't often that I had the house all to myself. My mother had taken my brother to Houston to a doctor that weekend, and my grandmother had stepped across the street to Miss Rosetta's house.

"Behave yourself," she mumbled, going out the door. "Little children need to be watched. You can't let them out of your sight for a second, or they'll climb on top of the house and fall off or electrocute themselves or eat poison or bite the dog or get stolen by a stranger or start thinking they can cook and burn themselves up."

The winter before, I'd nearly burned the house down, dragging curtains over the heater as I went from window to window trying to see something. Setting the house on fire was an accident, I thought, every time my grandmother brought it up. Could have happened to anyone. I didn't keep bringing up the time she set a grease fire on the stove and I had to help her put it out. In fact, I never told anyone about it, and not because she threatened to spank me if I did.

Distracted by the sound of a baby crying, I listened to the radio with less than full attention. I heard the baby cry again. My favorite time of the week having been disturbed, I got up, put on my fuzzless slippers, and went to the window. Careful not to let the fabric touch the potbellied heater, I pulled back the curtain. Hearing another kind of cry—a woman's scream—I peered through the frosted window. Frantically, I wiped the glass until the edge of my hand went numb and I could see. Our next-door neighbor's toddling baby dropped a jar of something and collapsed in the yard between our houses. Wrapped in a towel, his mother ran barefoot out of the house across the frozen ground and picked up her baby.

By the time I grabbed my coat and ran out, my grandmother and the rest of the neighbors were there, too. "Call a doctor," the woman cried, holding the child close. "My baby drank stove oil while I was taking a bath! I only left him alone for a second."

Up with the Chickens

Mr. Hines's rooster made the first sound heard on Candy Hill every morning that I can remember as a child in the 1950s and 1960s.

On one particular summer morning before my eleventh birthday, seconds after sunlight shattered a dark gray sky, I wanted to wring that rooster's skinny neck. I'd just dropped off to sleep after a fitfully sweaty night. The blades of a tiny fan in front of an open window, still slapping at stale hot air, hadn't cooled me through the night but had managed to keep mosquitoes from settling long enough to bite.

When the rooster's shrill voice cracked, I pulled the pillow over my ears and imagined the big, arrogant bird's head thrown back, a swag of skin under his neck swinging back and forth and his tail feathers stiff, as he strutted around listening to other roosters in the neighborhood join his racket.

Chickens were common on Candy Hill. Some families harvested vegetables from gardens on the sides of their houses and in their backyards raised chickens for eggs and meat. Roaming the neighborhood daily, chickens ventured far from their nesting places in the morning. Brown, black, red, gray, dingy white, and speckled chickens ran down the middle of a dirt road a few feet ahead of a car or waddled across drainage ditches or crossed someone's yard, as they wandered home late in the evening. Although Mother's Baby Ben clock usually sounded its alarm before the roosters cried, her clock had failed a few times while the Candy Hill roosters never had.

The morning after my sleepless night, everyone in our house except me was already up. The soft murmur of conversation around the breakfast table, along with the aroma of fresh coffee and bacon drifting from the kitchen, annoyed me. I was glad to hear the door close behind my parents as they left for work but saddened to hear the sound of my grandmother's voice calling me to get up.

"Laying in a bed too long when they're not sick makes people lazy," said my grandmother, standing in the bedroom doorway.

"Mr. Hines's rooster makes me sick," I said. "I hate roosters!"

"Roosters have a job to do," my grandmother said.

"I wish Mr. Hines would kill his old rooster," I said.

"You need to be more like that rooster."

"He's the one starting all the noise," I argued.

"That rooster is never late," she said softly.

"I wish Mrs. Hines would fry him up in a pan!"

"That rooster never complains," my grandmother said.

"She could serve him for supper!" I said.

"And the rooster never makes excuses."

"I'd eat his legs."

"When you grow up," my grandmother said, "you'll do fine if you do your job as well as that rooster does his."

Mrs. Jackson

Mrs. Jackson was walking home from work. I'd been sent to the store for a loaf of Butter Crust bread, four white potatoes, and two large onions. My mother was making liver and gravy for supper. No one could get me to eat liver! But I'd make a meal of smooth, dark-brown onion gravy over fluffy mashed potatoes, fresh mustard greens on the side, and a hunk of buttery cornbread.

Walking several yards behind Mrs. Jackson, whose face was tilted slightly toward the sky, I admired the fit of her red and yellow printed dress, snug at her small waist and flared at the hem. The gently scooped neckline was adorned with red ribbon trim. Straight shoulders and arched back supported her supple body. Studying her strides—which seemed to be planned for maximum grace despite the uneven gravel footing—I copied Mrs. Jackson's walk, matching my own steps to hers.

Walking in her trail, I could smell her flowery perfume and see her shiny tresses, garnished with Royal Crown hair dress. As many early Saturday mornings as I'd been to the Jacksons' house to play, I'd never seen Mrs. Jackson's hair undone. It was always elegantly arranged in a French twist, with curls framing her forehead and dainty pearls dangling from her earlobes. What style!

Candy Hill women created their own vogue, which did not come from a Paris runway, New York department stores, fashion magazines, bottles of expensive fragrances, or packages on store shelves. With little money for extravagances, proud and independent Candy Hill women used what they had to enhance their enviable, unpretentious charm. In 1961, all beauty products available in Bryan stores were manufactured for pale skin. Some mail-order houses listed in the backs of offbeat magazines offered one or two shades of makeup for black skin. Neither of those sources coordinated with Mrs. Jackson's soft caramel complexion, one being too light and the other too dark. So she bought both and mixed her own perfect shades of honey and cinnamon and used a deep coral for her lips.

Mrs. Jackson turned into the grassless yard of the tiny unpainted house she shared with her four children—Dora, Ed, Cleo, and Rose Marie. Her son, Woodrow, had gone off to college the year before. Her daughter Gloria and another son, both married, lived nearby, and her other girls lived in San Antonio.

Walking into her yard, Mrs. Jackson picked up some trash. I waved to her. She dropped the trash in a can beside a tree in her yard and waved back to me, smiling and warming my insides before she went into the house to start her family's supper.

Mr. Mason

Elderly Mr. Mason and his twelve-year-old grandson Stanley turned soil that winter day for next spring's vegetable garden in the vacant lot beside their neat yellow house on the corner of Pierce and Bradley. From the window of the playroom Mr. Mason had built onto the house for his grandchildren, Cynthia and I watched them shovel dirt, turn it over, and break up the clods.

Mrs. Mason, my grandmother, and other women in the neighborhood canned and preserved vegetables, made jams and jellies from fruit picked off trees growing in their yards, and sewed the family's clothing. Wearing a lace shawl around her slender shoulders, Mrs. Mason was in the kitchen, baking the second batch of gingerbread and stirring up a pitcher of powdered milk for the crowd of children at the house playing with her grandchildren. Dainty lace curtains at dining room windows and matching lace tablecloth demonstrated her love of the fine fabric. The rest of the immaculate house was cozy with wood furniture, paintings on walls, and soft-pillowed sofas and chairs.

My playmate, Cynthia, Mr. and Mrs. Mason's ten-year-old granddaughter, lived there, along with her mother, her brother, two aunts, and several of their children, including Stanley. Cynthia's mother and two aunts worked, while their elderly parents looked after the children. In a similar grouping, I lived with my grandmother and my parents. My grandmother kept the house and looked after me, while my parents worked. Like the Masons', our small house sometimes swelled to hold an assortment of displaced relatives and even friends who needed temporary housing. There were times when our house fed and slept as many as ten people.

That pattern was common on Candy Hill in the 1950s and 1960s. Many of our neighbors, restricted to subsistence wages for menial work, earned hardly enough for housing and food if several generations of people didn't live under the same roof and contribute to the household.

"I won't let my people live in the street," my grandmother always said. "Unless, of course, they're too sorry to help themselves and just don't want to do any better. In that case, the street is where they belong."

On Candy Hill, it was unheard of for someone to be homeless, hungry, and without clothes. We were too proud to let our neighbors suffer.

Miss Parthenia

I stood on the steps at Walton's Grocery Store, watching Miss Parthenia—neatly dressed in a soft cotton print dress, with two yards of silvery braids circling her head.

During springs and summers in the 1950s and 1960s, Miss Parthenia's home resembled an enormous bouquet of life and color. Around the edges of her property, miniature blossoms sprang from succulent ground-hugging plants. Her yard looked like a lush, green, shaded tropical forest from *National Geographic,* with soft grass, flowers, blooming shrubs, and elephant-ear leaves draped from the corners of her crisp white house.

Parthenia Victoria Harris moved to Bryan in 1919 from Calvert, Texas, with her husband, Willie Earl Harris, and their four young daughters, Helen, Edna, Corrine, and Katheryn. Helen Harris Simpson, the oldest and last surviving daughter, who still lives in the Harris home, was only seven at the time of the move. After the death of her husband, Miss Parthenia made a living teaching piano lessons from 1920 until 1950, traveling the countryside as a church musician, altering ready-made clothing, and designing and sewing custom dresses.

"But my mother always had time for us," I once heard her daughter Helen say. "She also helped to raise a lot of other neighborhood children. People were more involved with each other back then. We had a sense of community and responsibility to each other that's lacking today. And she really believed in education. She made sure that all of us graduated from the eleventh grade. That's as high as school grades went back then. Diplomas read 'Bryan High School,' but it was really Bryan Colored High School (later Washington Elementary School). Then we all went to college. I didn't finish, but, being the oldest, I worked and helped my mother to send my little sisters, and they finished."

While I admired Miss Parthenia's yard, she straightened up from tending a flower bed, turned, and waved to me, like she had eyes in the back of her head. During my childhood, all the older Candy Hill women seemed to have eyes in the backs of their heads. From the time I started walking until the time I started driving a car, I never got away with anything.

I saw Miss Parthenia's lips moving but couldn't hear what she was saying—probably something like "You be a good girl" or "You'd better be making good grades."

"Yes, ma'am," I called, waving before going into the store.

Voyage to America

Before Fred took the boat from China nearly one hundred and fifty years ago, he had already learned things that people in Brazos County didn't know back then—things like fancy fighting with his feet and hands that could break bones or even kill with one blow, and new ways to cook rice other than boiling it and burying it under chicken gravy.

I knew Fred well through the stories I heard his granddaughter tell in the 1950s, when I was a little girl. She said that her grandfather called himself Fred because the people in his new home couldn't seem to pronounce his old name. Once in America, Fred traveled to Texas when it was still the frontier, married a slave woman, and raised a brown-skinned family that would have gone unnoticed in our community if not for Fred's distinctive eyes. I knew people in Robertson

County with eyes like Fred's, but their grandfather was from Japan.

Fred's granddaughter's stories squeezed me under the ship's main floor and into dark, damp, flat quarters where the ceiling was too low to sit up. Rocking and swaying from side to side, my imaginary ship made me queasy, while imaginary companions threw up on each other. Inside her stories, my own lungs labored, as the air in the hole became thick with body odor and heavy with human excrement. I felt myself growing faint from the lack of something fresh to breathe. Fred's granddaughter said the vessel ran short of food and drinking water. Before long, everyone who wasn't starving or dying of thirst was ill. Infections caused by unsanitary conditions, and by bites and stings from the ship's animals and insects, claimed the youngest first, then the elders. My knees weakened as I thought of that little Chinese boy watching the decayed bodies of his family being thrown over the side of a ship in the middle of the night. When he reached the shores of freedom, Fred was herded with hundreds of others into detention centers, concentration camps, plantations, factories, and similar places of servitude.

When I heard my grandmother calling me home for dinner, I stood up, feeling guilty for my own good fortune, and walked the short distance to the safety of a home filled with people who took care of me.

The Dewberry Patch

I hated the dusty, bittersweet flavor of dewberries wrapped around gritty little seeds that stuck between my teeth.

"Come get the bucket," my grandmother called to me through the open kitchen door. "Go pick some dewberries from our side of the fence. Don't pick on the other side. I'm going to make a cobbler."

"Yummy," I moaned, walking slowly to the door to get the berry bucket. My grandmother was very sensitive about property lines and not intruding on the neighbors. I believe her motivation was rooted in her selfish desire for privacy.

"Did you say something?" she asked.

Admitting would have been a mistake.

My grandmother stared at me without blinking, handed me the pail, and let the screen door slam. I headed for the dewberry patch. Only one thing annoyed me more than eating those musty wild vine berries, and that was picking them. My grandmother didn't like picking berries any more than I did, and she hadn't picked one since I'd been old enough to do it. Berries grew on vines along yard fences, and almost everyone in the neighborhood nurtured peach and plum trees in their yards. In a little water and lots of sugar, fruit and berries were cooked until tender and syrupy sweet. The addition of flour dumplings and a buttery crust created a cobbler.

In the 1960s, before everything was prepackaged in a box or purchased at the take-out window of a fast-food restaurant, most Candy Hill grandmothers still made fruit turnovers, cobblers, pies, jams, jellies, and preserves from fresh berries and fruit. In fact, grandmothers cooked the meals, did housework, mended clothes, washed, and disciplined children. Because Candy Hill fathers were mostly absent in those days and the ones who were around earned so little, most of the mothers in my neighborhood were forced to work outside the home, while most white mothers across town were still housewives. Working mothers guaranteed grandmothers' active positions at home. Most Candy Hill homes had at least one grandmother; some had two. And no one wondered what to do with them or where to put them.

I stepped lightly into the dewberry patch. The trick was to collect as many berries as you could from one spot, without upsetting the thorny dewberry vines. Injuries from the petite thorns on the dewberry vines were not as painful as those made by spears of a rosebush or spikes and needles of some cactus varieties. But dewberry vines could be very deceptive.

The first couple of dewberries I picked were so ripe they burst between my fingers. Disgusting thick, warm purple juice ran down my arm. I flung it away and tried to take a step to change my position. Before I noticed, those sneaky dewberry vines had crept up and attached themselves to my legs. Nearly invisible thorns inflicted a thousand microscopic wounds to my skin.

"Fill the bucket," my grandmother shouted from the kitchen.

Melissa from Mississippi

All grownups on Candy Hill were suspicious, especially of people they hadn't known for very long, and particularly of people like my new friend Melissa and her family from faraway Mississippi.

"Better to watch your back than to find a knife sticking out of it one day, like your Aunt Effie's boy," said my grandmother, looking up from a sink full of mustard greens she was washing.

"Melissa's not like that," I said.

"What would an eleven-year-old child know about people from Mississippi?" she asked. "I don't want you bringing somebody here who is likely to pick up and walk out with some precious little treasure your mother worked hard and saved to buy."

My grandmother's meaning was clear, and I knew she could be right. Another of my playmates, whom I'd trusted and defended, had come every day for a week and taken whatnots from our living room on her way out the front door when I wasn't looking.

"Even some of your own kin can't be trusted," said my grandmother. "Remember that time I gave you a dime, and I tied it up in the corner of a lace handkerchief?"

How could I ever forget that? She'd repeated the incident regularly enough and shamed me about it since it had happened. And I was only three years old! "Your cousin came by, pretending to play with you," she said. "You turned your back! She stole your dime and left the handkerchief on the porch."

What's that got to do with Melissa? I thought.

"Better grow some eyeballs in back of your head," she sighed, dousing the greens into the water. "That's the only way you're going to survive in this evil world!"

"Huh?"

"Don't you understand anything?" she asked, looking up at me. "Don't you know you can't trust but a few people in your whole life? Some mean well, but out of weakness they let you down. Others mean harm right from the start."

"Everybody doesn't live like that," I whispered. "Do they?"

"Mostly those coming down from slaves do," she said absently, concentrating more on her greens now than our conversation, which I sensed was just about to end. So I listened carefully. "I don't trust anyone who comes down from old plantation politics. Masters getting slaves to trick other slaves for a scoop more of beans or the privilege of not having their children sold away from them. And later, when there were no more plantations, used-to-be masters getting used-to-be slaves to trick one another for a little dab of this or a little piece of nothing much."

As usual, what my grandmother said didn't make perfect sense to me at the time. Later, reflecting, I realized that only four generations separated me from slavery. And each link had passed down a simple inheritance of survival, which begins with eyeballs in the back of my head.

The Landlady's House

I knocked. Our landlady didn't answer. Maybe she's in the kitchen and didn't hear me, I thought, looking at the roses by the porch. Their poignant aroma, a funeral-home smell—thick in my nose, mouth, and throat—forced tears to my eyes. Darker than fresh blood, the huge roses were the deepest red I'd ever seen growing on a bush or in a bed or flower box. The lush, dewy petals were edged in what looked like ribbons of black satin. Straining their thorny stems, clinging to a battered trellis by a window, the roses climbed onto the roof.

My grandmother said our stingy landlady stole the rent and never repaired the shacks or installed indoor plumbing. I knocked again. Still she didn't answer. Rust dust tickled my nose, now pressed against the screen door as I peeked through broken wires. I knew I should leave the penny for the pail of water in the tin can on her porch, like all her renters did. But I set the bucket down and cupped both hands around my eyes for a look inside.

For two years, since the day she called me evil, I'd felt contempt for the landlady. Built like a sack of flour, she was walking down the road with a Bible under her flabby arm when she saw three-year-old me, dancing up a cloud of yard dirt to fast-tempo country and western music from our next-door neighbor's radio.

"I wish Christine would turn that radio off," my grandmother said, glancing up at our neighbor's window from the porch where she was sitting while she separated rocks and dirt clods from packaged dried pinto beans, which she tossed one at a time into a pan. "That twanging makes me crazy."

In the 1950s, radio in Bryan, Texas, was dominated by country voices whining about lovers they'd lost and wished they had back. Blues singers whining to wailing guitars about the same thing could be heard on black radio stations, KCOH or KYOK, from Houston, a hundred miles south. T-Bone Walker, Big Mama Thornton, Gate-Mouth Brown, and others also scratched their way out of Nashville, Tennessee, late at night, when Randy's Record Shop, a mail-order establishment, was spinning blues. In the 1960s, Joe Daniels, a local blues singer–organist–band leader, got a radio slot playing the rhythm-and-blues recordings of Ray Charles, James Brown, Etta James, Bobby

"Blue" Bland, Little Ester, and others on Saturday afternoons, while advertising such things as fryer specials for places like the downtown Humpty-Dumpty Grocery. Until juke-joint owners ran out of beer, sweaty couples slid across gritty concrete to the low-down dirty sounds rising from Pete Banana's jukeboxes.

The landlady stopped in the road, shook her head, and watched me turn in circles, kick up my heels, clap my hands, and laugh to the beat of the music. "Fast little thing y'all raising up."

"Morning to you, too," said my grandmother.

"Never seen a thing like her," she said, shaking her Bible at me.

"Uh-huh," said my grandmother, not looking up.

"Can dance," the landlady scolded. "Bet she can't pray."

I dropped to my knees in the dirt, clamped one eye shut, positioned the other eye on her, and recited the Lord's Prayer perfectly, right to the Amen.

"That's a scary thing," she whispered. "Evil, too."

I hadn't forgiven her for calling me evil. For two years, the neighborhood had laughed at what I'd done. Angrily, I knocked again, discovering that the door was unlatched. No one on Candy Hill locked the door in the 1950s. Filled with second-hand, hand-me-down, mismatched, makeshift, given or thrown-away furnishings, the houses I regularly visited had nothing in them worth stealing.

I knocked again. If anyone on Candy Hill owned valuables, no one knew it. They kept them in their pockets and bosoms or pinned to underwear. Uncle Fred wore a money belt. Women reached in their bosoms for money to pay at the neighborhood store, back of the vegetable wagon, or trunk of the salesman's car. But never at church! On Sundays, the purses—patent leather, lizard, suede, and fancy cloth—emerged from closets, trunks, and under beds.

I opened the door and walked in, hoping to find out something on her to tell that would ruin her reputation like she'd ruined mine. Beside her front door was the only telephone in Candy Hill after Miss

Mary had hers disconnected. Everyone with an emergency had used Miss Mary's phone until Sledge sneaked in one night, called long-distance, and ran up the bill. I stared at the cord slithering from a jagged hole in a wall.

Light from the only window filtered in through ill-fitting blinds with broken slats and folds of forgotten curtain fabric, heavy with undisturbed dust, rot, and smoke. We didn't have blinds. Water stains on the ceiling from a leaky roof formed the shapes of distorted faces clawing for freedom. High in the corners of the landlady's house, spiders had spun homes. Bugs nested in walls, beneath countless layers of sagging wallpaper. My eyes traveled down to a lone ashtray full of butts on a scratched table by an uncomfortable chair. She smoked?

A brown cuckoo clock, whose door was perpetually open, hung on the wall. The wooden fowl—frozen on the ledge of his tiny unkempt shack and laced in place by numerous strands of cobwebs—made no announcements of time. So that's a cuckoo clock, I thought. We didn't have a clock. My grandmother had a watch and chain her father had left when he died. She kept it in her pocket. Under the clock, a bureau leaned against the wall, its blistered surface hiding beneath a wilted doily. Atop the doily, a cluster of ornately framed, fading photographs formed a semicircle around an oil lamp with a blackened wick. There were no recent pictures in the group. We had old pictures of dead relatives and new snapshots of living ones, but none were framed. Even through haze on the glass, queer lighting in the ancient photographs exaggerated the pores in the skin of her dead kinfolk. Their postures were stiff, expressions serious. A panel of fake flowers behind one group of distant strangers made them appear to be dead people, artificially positioned to impersonate the living. The photograph reminded me of my cousin's funeral.

In the landlady's bedroom, a spotty mirror reflected light through a liquor bottle on the dresser below. She drank? A pot-bellied cast-iron wood heater with a bent black pipe sat away from one wall on a layer of unmatched bricks. I tried to imagine how warm that room must have been in winter, compared to our house, where the walls seemed like paper when the weather got the least bit chilly.

On the wall opposite the window was the lumpiest bed I'd ever seen. A pair of frayed slippers peeked from the shadows beneath the snowy bed linens. Where was she? I followed the delicious aroma of something cooking. In the kitchen, several pots on the wood-burning stove billowed steam. There were splatters of color all around the stove; pinto bean brown, dewberry purple, and squash yellow were easy enough to recognize.

Standing at the back door, beside a counter that held a dishpan and a bucket and dipper, I was shocked to see an outhouse. I'd always thought she had an indoor toilet, electric lights, a gas stove, running water, and a family. Wouldn't the Candy Hill people be surprised to know that she was so lonesome that she smoked and drank herself to sleep every night like they did and was just as poor? It would serve her right if I told!

When the outhouse door opened, though, the sight of her slightly bent figure emerging from the dark exterior room saddened me. I turned, making my way back through her house to the front porch. I grabbed the pail, went to the faucet and drew the water. Our landlady's kitchen table—set for one—summed up her lonely, irritable, interfering condition.

10

♦

After the Hill

Strange Hill

I was sitting on the front steps that Sunday afternoon in June, 1962, when Johnny and Marie Wiggins, both originally from New York, drove up in their white station wagon.

As the tires on the passenger side crushed weeds in a shallow ditch, I got up and walked down the steps, peering into the car. Not having seen them for nearly five years, I hardly recognized Terrel, who was about my age (twelve or so), sitting in the back seat with her two younger sisters. They had kept in touch through letters, photographs, and occasional visits when traveling through Texas from one military town to another.

In the early 1950s, Mr. Wiggins had been stationed at the Bryan Air Force Base—desegregated, along with the rest of the U.S. military, by President Truman in 1948. Every morning, Mr. Wiggins drove to the base. Every evening he drove back to the segregated, unpaved back streets of Bryan. Because of the necessity of living in this manner, many servicemen left their families at home rather than expose them to substandard housing, inferior education, inaccessible public facilities, and inadequate protection by law enforcement officers. Mr. Wiggins often came to our house for meals and, for small weekly payments, took a room in the home of our neighbor, Mrs. Rouse, a few doors down Dansby Street from us.

In 1951, when Mr. Wiggins arrived, most rental housing available on Candy Hill and similar neighborhoods in Bryan consisted of three-room shotguns without electricity or indoor plumbing; they had outhouses in back. One of the few decent rental vacancies in our neighborhood, a small yellow house on Henderson Street, was occupied by another military family, the Blackwells, from Mississippi. When Miss Rosetta married Mr. Gilbert and moved into his house around the corner on Twenty-First Street, a military family rented her house, complete with screened porch, formal dining room, and indoor plumbing.

Mr. Wiggins eventually sent for his wife Marie and the girls, as education was not an issue while their daughters were still so young. Candy Hill's stable, permanent families provided adequate female companionship for his young wife. And Mrs. Rouse's safe, well-kept, established, comfortable home accommodated them until Mr. Wiggins was reassigned to another base in a different town a couple of years later.

When they got out of the car, Mr. Wiggins looked up the street, breathed deeply, exhaled what resembled relief, and said, "In all of my life and all of my travels throughout the world, this is still the strangest place I've ever been."

A Change Is Gonna Come

I stared through the window pane at little wedges of blue, forming a mosaic pattern between bare brown tree branches.

"Everything's changing," my grandmother said to herself. "Never thought I'd live to see this day."

As usual, I had no idea where she was going with that thought. As her voice invaded the back of my brain, I was busy noticing that the tree branches, glistening in the morning sun, were beginning to squeeze tender green buds out of their joints.

"Everybody's fighting!" she said. "Everywhere in the world!"

I was silent. She wasn't looking for a response, I thought, noticing that those were the same branches that only a few weeks ago had strained under the weight of the season's last ice storm.

"Fighting!" she said. "Over a piece of land in the desert!"

Although my grandmother gladly answered any questions a child asked and listened if something was wrong, she didn't have conversations with children. She said they hadn't lived long enough to know anything worth talking about. So I was silent.

"And why fight over a swamp in China?" she went on.

Soon, I thought, those buds would give birth to leaves that would shade our yard. Then the flowers would appear, and the fruit trees would burst into the bees' song. I hummed softly.

"China sounds too much like Galveston to me," she said. "And I wouldn't take a piece of land anywhere around Galveston Island if somebody gave it to me, let alone fight over it!"

My grandmother—going on and on about all that stuff on the other side of the world—annoyed me.

"And voting!" my grandmother yelled. "People in this very country are still fighting over who can vote and who can't! Even here on Candy Hill, people can't vote."

Can't vote, I thought, stunned. I didn't know whether to break my silence or not. I had a question, and something was really wrong, so finally I asked, "Why can't Candy Hill people just walk up and vote for anyone they want?"

"For the same reason Candy Hill people would be put in jail for walking up to any water fountain and drinking any time they get thirsty," she said. "Or using any public restroom or trying to live anywhere besides Candy Hill."

My grandmother's ranting made me feel cramped and uncomfortable. I watched the winter of 1960 change into the spring of 1961 and we shed our heavy layers of boots, socks, sweaters, and warm underthings. Similar temperature changes occurred in nature each year, but that particular year blew in such a strong new political climate that it echoed even in my grandmother's voice.

Brother George

I was fifteen in 1965, when Brother George presented me a scholarship for winning a talent contest at Prairie View A&M College. "For her rendition of the song, 'Every Little Bit Hurts,' the winner is . . ." The disk jockey's big eyes bulged in my direction. I felt faint. My head began to swim. Sweating, panting, grabbing breaths out of the air, I needed more room in the waist of my white hoop-skirted evening gown that fit around my middle like sausage skin. What if the tips of my spike-heeled shoes got caught in the hoop? I'd complained to Mrs. Pruitt, my sponsor. I hated that dress, looking like a relic from *Gone with the Wind*. When Brother George called my name, I was afraid to move!

Black disk jockeys spoke with authority in those days. That unique and powerful group of music-industry professionals—revered by recording artists and aspiring performers—held in their hands the ability to break records, make stars, and earn millions for producers. Doing so meant spinning records on their radio programs over and over, until the buying public stampeded record stores demanding to buy that hot wax. That was in the days when the grooves of records were pressed into real hot wax, before corporate radio encroached on parochial markets and imposed itself on local tastes.

In the summer of 1966, I spent a great deal of time in Brother George's shadow. Those were the days when adults felt an unconditional responsibility to youngsters who were interested in their fields. And Brother George seemed to enjoy showing off his deejay business. My plan was somehow to use music to launch myself on a career away from Candy Hill. So, when I was sixteen, I convinced my parents and my grandmother to let me spend the summer with Uncle Evans in Houston, where I could be close to the action.

I loved tagging along when Brother George booked acts; reserved ballrooms; picked up records and tickets; attended rehearsals; met with promoters, artists, and photographers; went around town tacking promotional posters to lightpoles; frequented charity functions and athletic events; and hosted his daily four-hour midday radio show at the KYOK studio, in an old brick building on Preston Street in downtown Houston. Although he had no financial interest or business there, Brother George checked on construction at the Astrodome until the day it opened that summer and helped my little cousin Wayne get a job there.

I went with Brother George to meet Otis Redding before the "Summer Shower of Stars" at the Music Hall. Looking goofy in white sneakers, socks, and a white dress with a life-sized sunflower down the front, I walked into the hotel suite. Patty LaBelle, not much older than me, was there with her group, the Bluebelles, along with Sam and Dave and some band members. I was with Brother George when he attended a pre-show party for the Motown recording group, the Temptations, before they performed at the Palladium, a nightclub on Southmore Street in Third Ward. "Don't get out of my sight," Brother George always said when I went with him. "These are grown men, and you're just a kid."

Usually, when Brother George was on the radio, I'd watch him through the control-room glass for awhile, then I'd go upstairs to the ballroom and play the out-of-tune piano. Brother George told me that, in the old days, the radio station threw sock hops and talent shows up there on weekends for teenagers. I imagined the spotlight on me at the piano and remembered a day back in 1960, when I hurried home one cool evening from the house of my piano teacher, Mrs. King, to meet the piano man. For two years, I'd never missed a lesson. As a reward, my mother managed to squeeze out of our tiny budget money to buy a piano. Until I got my piano, the closest one was locked up tight behind the battered doors of New Zion Baptist Church several blocks away.

I didn't care that I'd never be able to sight-read complicated musical compositions or play classical concerts. What I longed for was the soul to play and sing like Ray Charles and my grandmother. The one time I heard her, I was stricken with jealousy. If I could play like her, I knew I could get a gig at Ray Barnett's Cinder Club on Dixie Drive or a contract on Don Robey's Peacock record label. I banged around on the piano for the next two years before my notes formed coherent musical phrases. Then, one summer day in 1962, just after my thirteenth birthday, I was practicing. My grandmother stood in the doorway and listened. For the first time, she wasn't frowning.

A virtuoso I was not. A musical genius I knew I'd never be. But I played well enough to get the attention of a preacher friend visiting my parents. He was looking for an accompanist for himself and the choir at his country church, a good place for me to spend my spare time, according to my parents. The preacher warned me not to expect the members of his little church to leap at the chance to sing with a piano. They'd never had an accompanist. I laughed to myself and hoped they wouldn't expect too much of me, since I'd never been an accompanist. The preacher went on to say they weren't prepared to pay much. Again, I laughed to myself. Any pay would be more than I had now. My parents didn't believe in allowances or giving me hard-earned bill money to throw away on junk.

After three years of playing piano at a country church with painted window panes and winning a high-school talent contest, I thought I was ready for the big time. But hanging out with Brother George was as close as I got to the big time during the summer of 1966. I followed him into Ray's hotel room, fragrant with fresh-cut flowers. Ray asked if I had come to audition as a singer in the Raylettes, his glamorous background vocalists. Although I knew my dad never would have allowed it, the mere thought of singing with the great Ray Charles caused my tiny world momentarily to stop turning! When Ray explained that he didn't have an opening, relief rushed through the room like a cool breeze, because I didn't want to hurt Ray's feelings by having to turn down his offer. My dad had warned me to drop all of the show-business foolishness before school started in September. Years later, I was embarrassed to learn that Brother George had set up the offer of an audition with Ray to make me feel important. Brother George, Ray, and I sat down to a club-sandwich lunch, and I hung on every word of two old-timers in a business where I longed to find a place. September, after all, was still a month away.

Time to Leave Candy Hill

The farthest thing from my mind in the 1950s, when I was growing up in the segregated Candy Hill neighborhood of Bryan, Texas, was attending Texas A&M University in College Station, less than five miles from my home. Texas A&M—not a university then—was the Agricultural and Mechanical College of Texas. People living in my neighborhood never dreamed of going to Texas A&M, which was (a) all-male, (b) all-white, and (c) all-military. Candy Hill was (d) none of the above.

I hadn't seen an Aggie until my mother took me to a movie at downtown Bryan's Palace Theatre. While my mother and I stood in the ticket line, I sneaked peeks at uniformed young men going into the lobby. They all looked alike to me. When my mother pulled me out of the theater and up the dark stairs that led to the balcony, I looked down on all those identical bald heads and wondered how they could tell one another apart.

Our next-door neighbor said that Aggies looked sort of like the boys who attended Allen Academy, where he worked as a cook, removed greasy stains from the kitchen floor with Coca-Cola straight from the bottle, and stole an occasional roll of toilet paper. Allen Academy was a military boarding school for boys from elementary school through the second year in college. I saw Allen boys every day and heard them, too. One block behind our house, the school was separated from Candy Hill by a ten-foot chain-link fence topped with barbed wire. Every morning of my young life, I heard their bugle call. "There's a soldier in the grass, with a bullet in his ———. Take it out, Uncle Sam, take it out." These lyrics Candy Hill kids sang to bugle call.

Allen Academy lost most of its military students and went civilian years ago. After losing most of its boarding students shortly there-after, the academy lost its historic location. The trustees sold the prop-erty to a federal prison.

I don't know who started calling Candy Hill by that name. I do remember outhouses in the neighborhood, because we had one be-fore we moved into our cottage on the corner. A neighbor of ours who worked with the outhouse crew was referred to as a candy man. Although I found it difficult to understand why someone who cleaned outhouses would be referred to as a candy man, I decided that some-one with a wry sense of humor connected the candy reference with the outhouse contents.

In the 1950s, the strong military influence in Bryan–College Sta-tion included a U.S. Air Force base west of Bryan, just off Texas High-way 21 near the Brazos River. The main function of the base was to train African-American pilots. Many servicemen lived in or near Candy Hill. My mother's cousin was married to a serviceman stationed at the base. He and his family lived across the street from us in Miss Rosetta's house, until her marriage to Mr. Gilbert broke up and Miss Rosetta moved back home, going by her old name, Johnson, again.

I heard a serviceman say that housing was so poor in segregated Bryan that the base probably would have to move away. I don't know if his reason was accurate, but I do know that the federal government systematically began closing portions of the base in the 1960s, until it became a deserted relic of cracked runways. Texas A&M since has purchased the site, restored the buildings, and named it the Texas A&M Riverside campus.

During the 1950s, the only people I knew who went regularly to Texas A&M's main campus in College Station were janitors and some Kemp High boys from Bryan who worked as pin-setters before Texas

A&M's Memorial Student Center bowling alley had automatic pin-setters. My cousin Bubba, who set pins for awhile, said he got tired of diving away from balls thrown hard by overzealous bowlers who seemed to enjoy trying to hit him more than the pins that he barely had time to set up between balls.

My first visit to Texas A&M was in 1966. I went to the chemistry department to get assistance with my eleventh-grade science competition. Stiff-bodied, uniformed male students seemed to be marching when they were walking. Boot heels clicking on concrete gave me the creeps. The matches I made for my science project exploded in the judge's face and caused hysteria in the gymnasium of the all-white Stephen F. Austin High School in Bryan.

When I graduated from high school, there were a few women attending Texas A&M, mostly professors' wives or daughters. Although a couple of cute black guys from Houston were attending, for me the school held little mystery or appeal. After graduation in 1967, I took a contract singing jingles for a San Antonio company, sang in night-clubs, released a record, and attended San Antonio College. In 1968, I joined a rock band, occasionally sang studio backup for country-music star Mickey Gilley, met and married a gospel singer and guitar player, had a daughter in 1970, divorced in 1971, became a studio musician for Brunswick Records in New York, sang studio background for crooner Jackie Wilson, and toured the British Isles with my cousin, Johnny Nash, on his famous "I Can See Clearly, Now" tour.

By 1973, at age twenty-four, I was weary of fast living and producers saying I was past my prime. Music had provided a good living and a good time and most of all had taken me away from Candy Hill to places I'd only read about before. But I'd had enough, and I'd seen too many tired, washed-up performers who couldn't get a gig if the sky was raining gigs. I knew female performers who had to take work as exotic dancers or worse. I knew old performers who relinquished the stage to fresh talent, played for small purses, or chanced a piece of admission tickets. I panicked, thinking about performing 350 nights a year like some did. I worried about being able to support my child if bookings dried up; and I didn't know how to make anything but music.

Realizing the instability of my life, I left New York and went back to Bryan, with college on my mind. Texas A&M would not have been my choice, had it not been so convenient. And at four dollars per semester hour, a better price was not to be found. Knowing there were many things I didn't want to do for a living, I wasn't about to spend four years at a school I didn't like learning to do something I knew I'd hate. Observing events from a distance had made my life seem more like research than living, so I enrolled as a journalism major. In most of my classes, I was the only woman. During my first two years, I could go to school for days and see fewer than ten female students. From the time I began school until I graduated in 1977, I saw no other African-American women, recall having one class with an African-American football player, and went for months without seeing a black face unless I caught a glimpse of myself passing a window glass.

Although I grew up with doors closed to me, my family did not allow me to excuse myself from trying. They gave me hope that I would open some doors. Over the years, life on Candy Hill has changed very little. And, unfortunately, those slight changes have not been for the better. Drugs and gangs have moved in, eaten away at the heart of the neighborhood, and demoralized the people. There are two escape routes—prison and the grave.

I see reflections of my young, wounded soul in the eyes of Candy Hill children as they walk past the federal prison that faces their homes. But they have no old folks at home, passing wisdom or even a plate of home-cooked potatoes at the dinner table. Instead, kids eat meals from different chicken boxes at different times, walk the streets high, and get the urge now and then to hurt someone. Ignored and left to stew unnoticed in dangerous juices, some Candy Hill children show no allegiance to institutions of any kind and never think about being alone in a world outside of Candy Hill.